THE GREATFULNESS GUIDE

Praise for *The Greatfulness Guide*

'What a great book! *The Greatfulness Guide* is a much-needed road map to help us through these challenging times.'
— Tom Cronin (Coach, Speaker and Author of *The Portal*)

'A must read! *The Greatfulness Guide* set us off on a fun and thoughtful journey about who we are and how we can train our minds to be comfortable in our own skin and be our best selves. The 'power of yet', listening to your inner coach and the importance of self-care are just a few of the keepsakes from our trip.'
— Greg (parent to Jack, aged 11)

'Wow, this book is life changing. It's really helped me understand how my mind works and has given me the confidence that I can overcome any future challenges.'
— Matt (aged 12)

'If only I had this book as a teenager. Realising the power of the mind but also how to manage it is invaluable to kids and adults alike. An absolute must for any parent and their kids.'
— Dan (parent to 3 children, ages 13, 9 and 4)

'As an educator, I feel that this book is an amazing tool to assist kids of all ages navigate their way to adulthood.
It's so user friendly and realistic. The perfect resource to build happy, resilient children who know themselves inside out.
A must buy for all parents!'
— Stephen (Teacher, Grades 5 and 6)

Next level
thinking

THE GREATFULNESS GUIDE

HOW TO THINK
NOT WHAT TO THINK

JACQUI JONES

murdoch books

Sydney | London

Published in 2021 by Murdoch Books, an imprint of Allen & Unwin

Murdoch Books Australia
83 Alexander Street, Crows Nest NSW 2065
Phone: +61 (0)2 8425 0100
murdochbooks.com.au
info@murdochbooks.com.au

Murdoch Books UK
Ormond House, 26–27 Boswell
Street, London WC1N 3JZ
Phone: +44 (0) 20 8785 5995
murdochbooks.co.uk
info@murdochbooks.co.uk

 A catalogue record for this
book is available from the
National Library of Australia

A catalogue record for this book is available from the British Library

ISBN 978 1 92235 131 9 Australia
ISBN 978 1 91166 814 5 UK

Cover and text design by Lana Daubermann
Typesetting by Lana Daubermann
Design manager: Kristy Allen

Printed and bound in Australia by McPherson's Printing Group

10 9 8 7 6 5 4 3 2 1

 The paper in this book is FSC certified.
FSC promotes environmentally responsible,
socially beneficial and economically viable
management of the world's forests.

To those people who have been a part of my journey so far, thank you. Particularly my mum, dad and sisters, who have always been there for me.

A special thank you to Rhodri, Samuel and Ella, my constant travelling companions. I love this adventure that we are on together and can't wait to see where it takes us next.

To my wonderful nieces and nephews, Olivia, Eliza, Nicholas, Annabelle, Max, Harri, Casi and Morgan, thank you for the joy that you bring to my life and the lives of your extended family.

To the team at Murdoch Books thank you for making this such a positive experience. Being my first book, I really had no idea what to expect and feel truly blessed to be working with such wonderful people. Special thanks to Lou, Libby, Justin, Kristy, Lana and Sarah for your support, talent and wisdom.

To the two Kates that made this all possible, thank you. You have shown me what wonderful things that can happen when women empower women.

Finally, this book is dedicated to children everywhere; may your life be a wonderful adventure!

Why I wrote this book...

I finished writing the first draft of this book at the end of 2019.

My original plan was to write a book that could help young people understand the power of their mind. My motivation was simple: I would write the book that I never had available to me when I was kid!

I also wanted to make this book an adventure for young readers and decided to take them on a journey through the skies. Little did I realise that plane travel, and actually all types of travel, were about to go through one of the biggest challenges of all time. In March–April 2020, the world as we knew it was literally shut down due to COVID-19 and travelling was no longer an option. Everybody's journeys came to an abrupt halt as we tried, on a global scale, to stop the spread of the virus. It was like one day the planes were buzzing in the sky and we were all busy living our adventures and then the next day—BAM!—it was suddenly taken away.

The pandemic has impacted us all in some way. No one planned for this to happen; no one really saw it coming and it's times like these that people start to question, 'What is this all about?' I would love to be able to give you a straightforward answer, as I'm sure your parents would, but unfortunately, there are no easy answers. What I can say is that what we are experiencing is a shift. This challenge is a lesson for all of us, adults and children alike.

I have no doubt that you really started to miss 'stuff' when you were asked to self-isolate, things like team sports on the weekend, hanging out with your friends at school or even just going to the park. Things that you have been able to do in the past without really giving it too much thought. Sometimes we don't realise how much we value something until it is taken away from us, or could be taken away from us at any minute. We can take things for granted without even realising it. Sometimes it takes a challenge like this to help us understand what is important to us; this is the shift that I am talking about. What the pandemic did was force many of us to stop and pay attention to what is really important: friends, family, good health and freedom of choice became the focus for many people.

Which brings us back to why I wrote this book. Many years ago, I took my mental health for granted. I just assumed that it was **'FINE'** and that I didn't have to do anything to take

A WORD ON 'FINE'

When you hear someone say that they are 'fine', do you ever really believe them? Many of us actually use this word when things are anything but 'fine'. We can use it as a shield of protection to help us to try to hide from the discontent that we may really feel. The next time you notice yourself using this word, I invite you to dig a little deeper. Use it as an invitation to look for new possibilities. How can things be better? Is there something that could help you to turn your 'fine' into 'fantastic'?

7

care of it. That is, until it was taken away from me. I experienced major depression and went through a very difficult time. However bad I felt at the time, though, I was determined to overcome it. Over many years, I taught myself how to take better care of my mind. I began to value my mental health and took positive steps every single day to make sure that I became mentally strong. I wanted to make sure that I could mentally, emotionally and physically cope with challenges when they came along, something that I had not been very good at when I was young. That's what this book is about—how to take good care of your mind and make the most of its amazing power!

One thing I have learnt over the years is that while we cannot control what happens to us, we can control how we respond. COVID-19 is the perfect example of this. None of us, not even the adults in your life, were able to control this situation. Throughout the challenge, I'm sure you saw many people react with fear, while other people reacted with strength and courage. In challenging times, we always have a choice. Do I react with fear or do I react with love? Do I let this experience shrink me or do I choose to allow this experience to help me grow? We always have a choice. That is the wonderful thing about being human: we really do get to decide.

At the end of the day, life really is a journey. It is an adventure that is filled with many wonderful, happy moments, as well as difficult times that sometimes feel like they will never end. However, they always do. It's important to recognise that nothing is permanent. Everything comes and goes, just like those planes in the sky. With each and every experience, there is an opportunity for us to learn. The pandemic has been one of those experiences. It has provided us with an opportunity to learn together on a global scale.

From this incredible challenge will come new inventions and new ways of doing things that will empower us to change. There will be new medicine, new protective clothing and who knows what else? Perhaps we will see a flood of new music or new books from people who chose to use their time in isolation to get creative! Despite all that has happened, the adventure will go on and our journeys will continue. Hopefully we can learn to appreciate what we have right now, the little things like being out in nature, games with our family or simply talking with our friends.

WITH THAT IN MIND, IT'S TIME TO TAKE OUR THINKING TO THE NEXT LEVEL.

THE JOURNEY

Part 2: On your way

Part 3: Preparing for landing

YOUR TRAVEL GUIDE

Hi, my name is Jacqui Jones and I am going to be your travel guide.

Are you familiar with **Mary Poppins**? She is the perfect English nanny, friendly yet firm, and the best thing about her is that she likes to use a little magic! Well, if Mary Poppins were to have a long-lost Australian cousin, I might just be her. Why?

1. I spend my days working with **children**. Most of the time you will find me travelling around to different schools with my own **bag of tricks**, teaching a program that I created called **GREATFULNESS**. And while Mary liked to use a bit of magic, I like talking about the **magic of the mind!**

2. I am also a **no-nonsense nurturer.** That means that while I genuinely care for you and want to see you **shine**, I also expect that you accept responsibility for yourself, regardless of age. I truly believe that you are capable of anything you put your mind to.

3. **I love adventure.** I've had years of experience choosing different paths to travel down, some good, some not so good. This is actually what makes me the perfect travel guide as I'm pretty good at **overcoming turbulence** and **dealing with detours**.

4 **I SEE YOU.** By that, I mean that I really do see how hard being a kid these days can be. There are so many different pressures on you and it can be hard to know which way to turn. That, my friend, is where I come in.

I'll let you in on a little secret. When I was your age (yes, it was a long time ago now!) I was filled with so many really **BIG** questions about life. The greatest challenge for me was knowing **WHO** had the correct answer and, to be totally honest, I kind of always felt like the adults in my life didn't actually have the answers. Have you ever felt like that? You may have been asking questions, hoping to get a clear explanation but no one was really able to provide you with a satisfactory answer? The real answer is that we are all still learning, even the adults. We simply don't have all the answers—but we can be willing to learn.

When I was your age, I really wished there was a book that I could turn to that could help me to understand some of this 'stuff' about life. Even now, when I speak to some of your parents, someone always says to me,

WOW

'I WISH I HAD KNOWN ABOUT THIS 20 YEARS AGO!'

So in a way, you guys are lucky. Not knowing all of this 'stuff' has led me to discovering many things about how the mind works and I am now writing the book that I would have loved to have read when I was your age. This book will hopefully help you to better understand the **magic of your own mind.** For example, did you know that your mind is one of your most powerful tools? Everything that you think, see, feel, and do is first filtered through your mind.

 ## Just think about that (excuse the pun!)

I feel truly privileged to be working with you. I hope that you can trust the guidance that I am going to share and put it into action in your own lives. You don't have to do everything straightaway, just start taking **little steps forward** and I guarantee that you will make progress.

Just keep reminding yourself throughout this book and throughout your life's adventure that no matter what happens:

YOU'VE GOT THIS!

STARTING POINT

Can you imagine your life being like one big, exciting journey? What an adventure that would be! That, my friend, is exactly how this book works. We are about to embark on a journey together that is going to be filled with lots of **new experiences** and **new knowledge**. What are we going to discover? Well, that is really up to you. I hope that this journey might open your mind to a new way of thinking about your life and help you to discover how to become the 'next level' you. It's almost like giving yourself permission to get an update. What would the 'next level' you be like? Have you ever taken a moment just to think about it? Like any good adventurer, you are also going to have to do some work throughout our journey. It's going to require you to move out of your comfort zone a little in order to discover what else is out there.

Have you ever been on a holiday? Can you remember the **feeling** before the holiday arrived? Do you recall those feelings of anticipation and not being able to sleep the night before because you were so **excited**? That's exactly how I want you to feel about your life. I want you to get so excited about your life that you literally **jump out of the bed** in the morning just to see what the new day is going to bring! Yes, life can be serious. Yes, life can bring unexpected challenges and worry. But I want you to understand that no matter what happens **you can do this**. You can live a life full of **adventure**, despite the challenges, and realise that actually the challenges are what help you to become a stronger, wiser version of yourself.

 YOU WILL LEARN THAT THESE EXPERIENCES ARE A BIG PART OF TAKING YOUR LIFE TO THE NEXT LEVEL BECAUSE THEY CAN HELP YOU DO THINGS DIFFERENTLY.

To make this serious topic a bit more fun, this book is filled with travel analogies—and lots of them!

If you have ever been to an airport to catch a plane then you probably know what I mean when I say that there is something so exciting about travel. So, are you ready to go on this journey together? I have a few travel tips before we get started.

WHAT IS AN ANALOGY?

An analogy is when you take an idea and compare it to something else that you are familiar with. For example, 'imagine your life like a journey'. Are you with me?

GOING UP!
Open your mind
to new possibilities

TRAVEL TIPS

(1) STAY CURIOUS – I know how curious you
are and that's a wonderful thing! As you
read through this book, there may be some
things that you want to question—things
that don't make sense to you right now
or that you might not agree with. That's OK.
All I ask is that you **stay curious.** Seek out
the answers if you want to, by talking to an
adult or doing some research on your own.
This book is meant to open the doors to
your life's adventure, so be open to where
this new information may take you. If you
finish this book with new questions, that is
a wonderful sign that you have started to
think differently.

(2) COMMIT – If you want to reach your
destination, it is usually a good idea to stick
to your itinerary. Flights might get delayed
and you need to be flexible but I want you to
commit to getting through this book. Make it
your mission to read it once, and then even
a second time. The more you are able to put
into this book, the more you will take away.

③ KEEP A TRAVEL DIARY – Take notes throughout your journey. You will have the opportunity to take part in lots of different activities so I recommend getting a blank notebook to do the suggested activities and record what you are learning. This isn't 'homework' but a fun way to put your new knowledge to use. You can make it like a travel journal and fill it up with anything that inspires you. Cut out pictures, draw a sketch, write in some quotes—basically include anything that makes you feel good. Make it a work of art!

Keep your eyes out for this icon. **Every time you see it, it is your chance to get writing or drawing.** Have a bit of fun with it all as well!

④ GETTING ASSISTANCE – It's OK to ask for help. If there are things that you don't quite understand, by all means have a chat with an adult you trust. Ask their opinion. Remember that they are still on their life's journey, so I bet they will have a few points worth sharing with you!

5 **PIT STOPS** – It's totally OK to take 'pit stops'. The beauty of this guidebook is that you can put it down and pick it up a few weeks later and it will still all make sense. Set your own pace.

6 **HAVE FUN** – If life is your biggest adventure, then you really should be having some fun. Yes, there are some very serious topics here **but** that doesn't mean you can't have fun learning about them and applying your new knowledge.

So, put a smile on your dial and LET'S DO THIS!

PART ONE:
BEFORE YOU GO

DISCOVER YOURSELF

Every **good explorer** knows that before you set off on an adventure you need to spend an enormous amount of time planning. So that's exactly what we are going to do: plan, prepare and do some research. Now, before you put this book down because I just mentioned the words 'plan, prepare and research', **stick with me!** This first stage of the journey can actually be loads of fun. What if we replaced those three words with something a little more interesting? How about ...

 ## PLOT, CONCOCT AND INVESTIGATE?

That's much better, don't you think? Let's **plot** your next move, **concoct** a plan and then **investigate** what other information is out there. This is where curiosity comes in because it's really about opening your eyes to new pieces of information and figuring out how that new information can help you. This is the work that we have to do **before** we can set off anywhere, and it's **absolutely essential** if we want to make the most of our journey together. So let's start investigating.

Curiosity keeps your eyes wide open.

YOUR ODYSSEY

I invite you to start thinking of your life as an odyssey.

WHAT EXACTLY IS AN ODYSSEY?

Thanks for asking! It can be defined as 'a long exciting journey'.

It's the most epic adventure you will ever go on and therefore it should be something to get excited about, not shy away from. There are a few other things to understand about an odyssey:

1. it's about the journey, so it's OK to not have it all figured out at this stage;

2. everyone's odyssey is going to be different, so just try to focus on your own;

3. there is no perfect way—**there is only your way**.

There is no right or wrong way of doing this. There are definitely a few things that you can do to help you make the most of your adventure but even if you choose not to do them, the journey is still going to happen. Let me say that again:

YOUR JOURNEY IS STILL GOING TO HAPPEN,

no matter how well or how little you have prepared for it.

There are so many people who get to the end of their odyssey and wish they could do it again because they feel they didn't make the most of it. I want to help you make the most of your odyssey, so I will be giving you lots of tools and tips to help you reach your final destination. Can you guess the final destination? It's not really a physical location.

The final destination is actually the process of discovering the 'next level' you—the version of you who is **living life to their fullest potential and making the most of every opportunity**. As your travel guide, I hope to help you have a **safe, healthy and wonderful odyssey**, a life lived with so much joy, happiness and adventure that it leaves others inspired to do the same.

Time to create! Go to the front page of your travel diary and draw a picture of the 'next level' you. What do you look like? What types of things do you love to do? Think big!

WHAT TO PACK

You need to pack the essentials, but be sure to leave room for all the new stuff that you are going to pick up on the way. **First rule of travelling:** always leave space to welcome in new 'stuff' and new experiences. For now, here a few items I would like to recommend:

We might hit some turbulence on the way or have a few detours, so we really need items like **courage** and an **open mind** from the start. Items such as a willingness to try and persistence will also be required to help you through any challenges. If you are running short on things like **self-love** and **gratitude**, don't worry. We will hopefully discover these, and many other things, on our journey together.

There are a few items that will probably make their way into your bag that we will also try to deal with throughout the journey, such as fear, worry and stress. If you know they are going to be hard to leave behind, it's OK. We will offload them when you are ready.

25

THE TRAVELLING TYPE

People travel for all sorts of reasons: to have an adventure, discover new cultures or to 'find themselves'. What type of traveller are you?

MISSION MAKER

You may have an important assignment or mission to complete and are happy to travel to achieve it.

THRILL SEEKER

You are keen to take part in anything exciting: especially if it involves physical risk!

SOUL SEARCHER

You have a desire to look for more meaning in your life. You feel like there is 'something more' and want to find it.

THE NOMAD

You are a wanderer, travelling from place to place. You are happy just drifting in between.

THE BLOGGER

Your journey is lived through social media. You care a great deal about getting the 'perfect' shot!

MY PHILOSOPHY

Perhaps you don't know what type of traveller you are yet. That's OK. At your age, there is still a great deal of 'figuring out' to do, and you probably have many more questions than answers. It is important to realise that over the course of your journey, **you will change.** You might start out as a Nomad, just wandering from place to place with no particular plan and then you might arrive at a location that nudges you towards becoming a Mission Maker. You might discover a project or assignment that sparks something within you and you get the feeling that you are just meant to work on it.

This book invites you to become aware of how you view the world and your own journey. Is your view helping you or holding you back?

MORE IMPORTANTLY, ARE YOU OPEN TO LOOKING AT THE WORLD IN A DIFFERENT WAY?

I believe that we are all here for a reason.

We have been given this opportunity to travel our own journey so that we can discover our **best selves** and ultimately **help others** to do the same. No one's journey is the same. We all have something different to offer, and part of the journey is discovering what it is that **YOU** have to offer the world. This is where the adventure should begin! You don't need to put pressure on yourself to try to figure out your reason for being here—this is part of your journey. All you need to do right now is be **open** and **curious.**

Oh, and let's not forget to have some fun!

You have a treasure chest within you.

WHAT'S OUT THERE?

WHAT IF...

Sometimes, when we ask questions such as, 'What is my reason for being here?' it can sound very serious. I'd like you to have a bit of fun with this, and approach it with a sense of topsy-turvy! Instead of asking yourself, 'What is my reason?', why not try changing it to 'What if?'. Ask yourself:

 ### 'WHAT IF THERE IS A SPECIAL REASON FOR ME BEING HERE?'

How does that make you feel? Some people, like the Mission Makers, may already know their answer but you may not. That's completely OK! If you can ask the question and then remain open and curious, you never know what you might discover. It might take another ten years of adventure before you feel like you have figured it out, but in the meantime, you can make it your mission to have fun discovering your true potential! Many of us are in the habit of comparing ourselves to others. We can look at the person next to us and think, 'Why do they have it all figured out?' Then we can feel bad about our own journey. While we humans are all seeking love, happiness and connection, we all have very different ways of finding those things. So just keep reminding yourself:

I AM EXACTLY WHERE I AM MEANT TO BE.

Because you totally are.

IS IT JUST A DREAM?

Forget travellers for a minute. Many of you might have a dream of something that you would like to do or be. You know, something deep within you that you rarely talk about because you're afraid that other people might laugh? It could be that you have a dream of becoming a writer, or an artist, or perhaps you want to represent your country in the Olympics? You might have a dream about helping Mother Earth or improving the lives of others.

The English Oxford Dictionary defines the word **dream** like this:

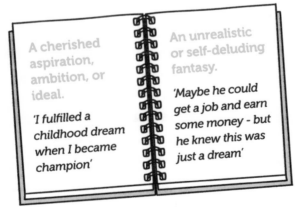

A cherished aspiration, ambition, or ideal.

'I fulfilled a childhood dream when I became champion'

An unrealistic or self-deluding fantasy.

'Maybe he could get a job and earn some money - but he knew this was just a dream'

So a dream can be either a **'cherished aspiration'** or **'an unrealistic or self-deluding fantasy'.** Wow, there is a big difference between the two definitions!

The first definition leaves you filled with hope, and then you read the second one and it's like, gulp, well, maybe I should just give up on my dreams. So, what do you believe? **Ask yourself now**. What do you honestly believe about having dreams? What stories have you been told? Have you always been told stories about people who had dreams and failed? You might feel it's too risky to dream. Or have you heard stories about those people who have had dreams and worked hard to achieve them?

I BELIEVE THAT OUR DREAMS ARE LIKE SEEDS. ONCE THOSE SEEDS ARE PLANTED, WE NEED TO LOVE AND NURTURE THEM SO THAT THEY CAN BLOSSOM.

Dreams take work! If we dare to dream but then don't do anything with them, what happens? Not much! It's then that a dream is more likely to become a 'self-deluding fantasy'. So, the key difference is action, which we talk more about later. For now, I want you to realise that **having dreams is a wonderful thing!** Allow your dreams to bring joy and purpose into your life.

What are the dreams that live deep within you? Go to your diary now and imagine that you have a treasure chest within you. What treasures are in there? They could be skills, talents, passions or hopes for the future. Write freely about what you find when you open your special treasure chest.

 Visit greatfulness.com.au/resources/ to download a free Treasure Chest meditation.

STORYTELLER

What if I told you that **you have the power to decide how this adventure proceeds**. Your life is your story, and you are the author. You get to decide who you want to be. You can play the role of the victim, the hero, the drama queen or the inspiring leader. Most importantly, when things don't seem to be going to plan, you can always keep coming back to how you want it to play out. You can rewrite the chapter at any time and get yourself back on track. If you think about the different books that you have read over the years, you will begin to recognise that there are all sorts of endings.

The possibilities really are endless. The only thing that limits you at this stage are your imagination and belief in your own abilities. Walt Disney, one of the greatest storytellers of all time, said it perfectly:

ALL OUR DREAMS CAN COME TRUE IF WE HAVE THE COURAGE TO PURSUE THEM.

To get you thinking about how you can create the most amazing story of your life, I want you to ponder these questions. You can write down the answers in your travel diary, or talk these through with an adult you trust.

1) What is the main role that I play in my story?

NOTE TO SELF:

THERE ARE NO RIGHT OR WRONG ANSWERS!

2) What do I love about myself?

3) What excites me about my life adventure?

4) What do I want to share with others?

BIG WIDE WORLD

Have you ever stopped to think about **how big the world actually is?** How many amazing places could you travel to? How many interesting people could you meet? **Then think about the Universe.** Earth is surrounded by planets and galaxies and who knows exactly what else!

I want you to try something. Read through the instructions and then give this a go.

Wherever you are, I want you to look up. What do you see? If there is a ceiling, I want you to think about that. Yes, the roof is keeping you safe but it's also stopping you from seeing what else is out there—it is keeping you in your comfort zone. If you can, head outside or to anywhere where there is no roof. Again, **look up** into the sky. What do you see? Is it an expanse of **blue sky** or perhaps there is a **sky full of stars?** Can you see any borders or endings or does it just keep on going and going?

There is a big, wide world **out there** just waiting to be discovered. Your life is meant to be filled with **wonder and awe**. To open yourself up to this, simply ask:

What else is out there for me?

WONDER

I grew up on a big farm in regional New South Wales, Australia. I used to love hopping into my bed at night and looking out my bedroom window into the **dark night sky bursting with stars** that would literally go on and on. It made me feel so connected, like I was part of this big, wide world in the most **magical, yet unexplainable way!** It also filled me with **curiosity**. Our house was located about 25 kilometres from Wagga Wagga, which meant that at night I could see the lights of the 'big city'. **I would just look at those lights and wonder** what the other people were doing in their houses and what their lives were like. I would wonder if anyone was looking at the same stars as me and I would also wonder: **What else is out there for me?**

WONDER
(verb)

to be filled with joy, excitement and childlike curiosity.

EMBRACE THE 'WONDER' THAT I KNOW IS WITHIN YOU.

Embrace the burning desire to figure things out, to go on an adventure and discover more about yourself and others. I want you to allow the excitement of a new day to put a smile on your face **every single day!** Wonder is an amazing feeling, so the next time you notice it, try to enjoy it. Can you allow your sense of wonder to guide you?

EQUIPMENT CHECK

UNDERSTANDING YOUR EQUIPMENT

Before we officially start the journey, we need to check our equipment. In particular, I want us to check one very important piece of equipment that we all have, but many of us don't know how to use it very well. **Do you know what it might be?** It is something that you use on a daily basis and, in most cases, works extremely hard for you. **It's your mind!** Perhaps you were thinking, **'Oh yes, my brain'** and that is the first lesson right there, to understand the difference between the brain and the mind. I like to explain it like this:

 YOUR BRAIN IS LIKE THE HARDWARE; YOUR MIND IS LIKE THE SOFTWARE.

Just imagine your brain being like a tablet and your mind are the apps that you have installed. Have you ever stopped to think about what programs or apps you have running? **Our programs are usually made up of our thoughts and beliefs.**

So, what does any of this have to do with your odyssey? Well, your programming is going to have a pretty huge influence on where you end up. I'll give you an easy example. Just say that you have come to believe that flying on a plane is dangerous and scary. Now, imagine that you are just about to board your plane but you can't. You are convinced that you can't do it and the thoughts inside your head are pretty loud: Don't do it!

If you don't board the plane, guess what? You have to change your plans.

Your thoughts are literally in charge of where you choose to go. What happens if you choose to get on the plane? Well, then you unlock the doors to unlimited possibilities.

THE MIND THAT OPENS TO A NEW IDEA NEVER RETURNS TO ITS ORIGINAL SIZE.

LUGGAGE LESSONS

Have you ever seen a baggage claim inside an airport, with people waiting for their bags to come through on the conveyor belt? Bags of all different types and sizes appear. You have the **old, beaten-up bag** that looks well-travelled and a little outdated and the new trendy type of bag that is all **shiny and compact.** Then there are backpacks and duffel bags, bags on wheels and even bags that you can ride! There are small bags, medium bags and then the oversized type that make you think,

 WOW, what on Earth's inside that?

I want you to think of your thoughts like all these different bags on a conveyor belt. Each bag represents a thought that travels through your mind. For example, the old, beaten-up bags might represent your old, worrying thoughts while the shiny new bags might represent your more hopeful thoughts for the future.

 DO YOU KNOW HOW MANY THOUGHTS THE AVERAGE HUMAN MIND HAS ON A DAILY BASIS? 50,000–70,000.

That's pretty amazing, don't you think? So just imagine standing there and watching 50,000 different

types of luggage come through, one by one. That's what we want to be able to do with our thoughts: observe them, just notice them passing by.

You see, we humans have a HABIT of clinging on to some of these thoughts, particularly the big, worrying ones. So we see that old bag coming through and we jump straight onto it and claim it as ours. Then that bag comes with us everywhere. It's even by our bed, keeping us awake when we are trying to go to sleep. We've had this old bag for such a long time, we don't really know how to leave it behind. Most of us have probably never even questioned it being there! Well, it's time for you to pay more attention to what luggage you lug around on a daily basis. How much excess baggage do you have?

The good news is that, just like with our luggage, we can replace and update our thoughts. We can train ourselves to let go of the old, outdated ones and upgrade to something more compact and efficient! We'll talk later about how we can actually do this, but first we need to look a little more at the **power of our thoughts.**

FACT OR FICTION?

Thoughts are powerful, but they are not all true. Just because we think something doesn't make it a fact! **Have you ever thought about this? (Pun intended!)**

I want you to really take this piece of information in because it's good news:

YOUR THOUGHTS ARE NOT FACTS!

We have this tendency to **believe** everything we think, but it's simply not the case. Take a look at the picture opposite. If you start at the top, you can see a thought leads to a feeling, a feeling leads to a behaviour and then the process will repeat itself. They might feel separate, but really they're such connected processes:

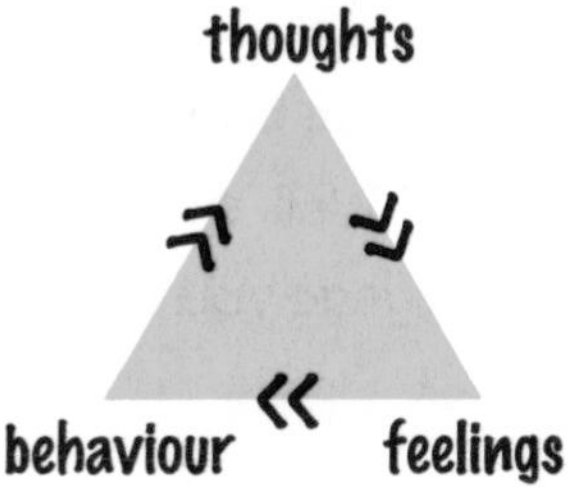

thoughts

behaviour   feelings

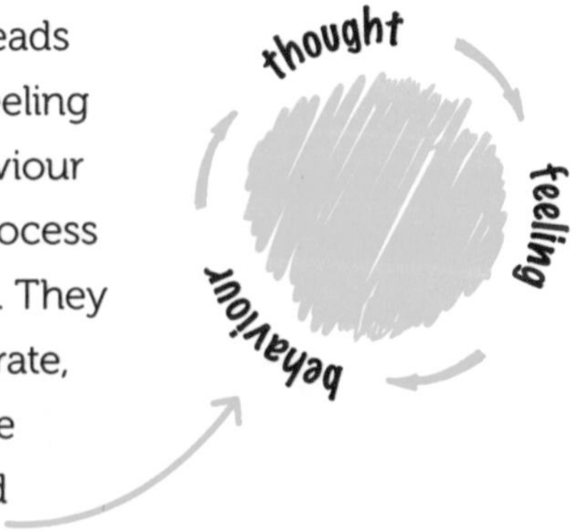

thought

feeling

behaviour

Just say that you have the thought: **'I am hopeless at maths'** and you have a big maths exam coming up at school. This **thought,** 'I am hopeless at maths' will most likely make you **feel** very nervous. On the day of the exam, you can feel **butterflies in your tummy** or your hands might be shaking. So now your body is not feeling great. Someone asks how you are getting on and you snap at them **'Just leave me alone, I'm fine!'**, which is your **behaviour.** They leave you alone, feeling hurt (as they were only trying to help) and now you have the new thought, **'Oh man, what's wrong with me?'** and you start feeling disappointed that you can't do anything right. At that point, you might even have a good cry, which again is your behaviour. Can you see how the process or cycle just keeps repeating?

 **If we think the same thought over and over, it becomes a belief.**

This is why our thoughts are powerful. They impact the way we feel and behave, every single day, even if they aren't actually true! So, my next question to you is:

 **WHAT DO YOU SPEND YOUR DAY THINKING ABOUT?**

Let's go back to our luggage example. What bags are you carrying around with you each day? Are they the **old, beaten-up bags** that are heavy and holding you back or are they **new** bags that you know keep you on track towards becoming your 'next level' self?

If the journey is about discovering your **#1 self,** it would make sense to start paying attention to your thoughts, right?

DID YOU KNOW THAT APPROXIMATELY 90% OF OUR THOUGHTS ARE THE SAME AS THE ONES THAT WE HAD YESTERDAY?

The good thing about our thoughts is that we can choose to change them at any time. All we need to do is pay attention to what is helping us and what might be holding us back.

Are your thoughts helping you or holding you back?

INVENTORY

An inventory is a list. This is the first thing I want you to try when it comes to recognising your thoughts— start making a note when you notice the same thought coming back again and again. **Just recognise that it's there.** It's a bit like standing back and noticing the same bag going around and around on the conveyor belt. The real trick is to notice the bag without claiming it as yours!

'Wow, there goes that old, worn out bag again.'

and then **choose to leave it there** rather than pick it up and take it home with you. When it comes to your thoughts, the first step really is just to notice what you are thinking about. Many of us don't really pay attention to the thoughts that are coming and going inside our head, and if we don't know what we're actually thinking about, how are we ever going to change them?

I'm not good enough.

You really shouldn't do that.

I am a failure.

This is going OK.

You've got this.

Seriously, not again.

Did you notice something there? There are more negative thoughts then positive ones. I have deliberately done this to help you understand that human minds have what is called a **'negativity bias'**. That means that we are more likely to look for what is going wrong as opposed to what is going right. I'll say it another way: we humans tend to have a lot of negative thoughts. Actually, they make up about **70% of our thinking**, but don't let that news ruin your day! I would prefer you to look at it this way: **'Wow, that's good to know!'**

THE NEGATIVITY BIAS IS OUR TENDENCY TO PAY ATTENTION TO ALL THE THINGS THAT ARE GOING WRONG, AS OPPOSED TO WHAT IS GOING RIGHT.

EXCESS BAGGAGE

If the first step is to become aware of what you are thinking about, one tool that can really help you do this is meditation.

Now for those of you who are tempted to stop reading right now, hear me out! What if I told you that some of the most successful people in the world meditate on a daily basis? Meditation is actually like

It's time to go to your diary and start your own inventory of your thoughts.

This will be a work in progress as it may take a little bit of time for you to start recognising the thoughts that come and go. I don't expect you to record 50,000 thoughts in your diary! But you can certainly start noticing if there are any thoughts that keep showing up, particularly the negative or worrying ones. All I want you to do is to become aware of the thoughts and write them down.

Many of us spend our time thinking about worrying things and don't even realise that's what we are doing. Later on, we will work our way through what to do with these worrying thoughts, because that is also very important and often the reason we try to distract ourselves from our thinking: we don't want to give them any attention because it feels too uncomfortable! But the first step is to notice what you are thinking about. Once you do this, we can then work towards helping yourself through the challenging thought.

filling yourself up with your own special rocket fuel. It literally is a superpower that we all have access to. Unfortunately, many of us don't do it. Why? Well over the years, I have heard all sorts of excuses (I mean, reasons!):

IT'S WEIRD...SO BORING...CAN'T DO IT!...I'M TOO BUSY!

Have you ever stopped to think of the reasons why you should give it a go? Here are just a few:

✓ improves sleep (yay!)

✓ reduces stress and worry

✓ helps us to manage our feelings

✓ helps us focus and concentrate

✓ leads to better decision-making

✓ improves creativity

✓ calms the mind

✓ boosts confidence

Rather than me try to convince you, I thought it might be useful to call in some help from a very special guest. Actually, you will hear from a few different special guests throughout this book so it might help to imagine these stories appearing on our inflight entertainment channel, **UP AND AWAY**. Each episode has been specially chosen just for you, to give you extra inspiration throughout your journey.

UP AND AWAY
with NOVAK DJOKOVIC

Q. Novak, who encouraged you to get started with meditation and visualisation, and what age were you when you started?

A. I grew up listening to classical music as a way of relaxing between my trainings. My first coach Jelena encouraged me to follow the path of visualisation, and I think I was quite a good student. I listened to music, I visualised lifting trophies and being the number one tennis player in the world. I was practising my victory speeches and making trophies out of cardboard box. I think it brought good energy and vibes to what I was doing. When it came to training, I was always a winner and I always had a bigger goal in front of me as a path to follow.

Q. What do you think are the three main benefits of meditating, for you?

A. It helps me stay connected with my inner self, my inner child. Life has a way of keeping us busy, stressed and always active, and meditation helps us slow down, remember that we have it all already within ourselves. That we are enough, we are divine and we are light. It keeps me grounded, helps me separate my voice from the voices around that keep asking me to be more, do more, have more. This way, I am close to myself and I am grateful to have learnt this early on.

Q. Do you have a special place where you like to meditate or is this something that you can do anywhere?

A. Nature. I love woods and parks. I always look for a 'special' tree, with strong roots and branches. I sit under the tree and meditate, then I hug the tree and—if possible—I love to climb it too!

Q. Has meditation or visualisation helped you in your career as a tennis player?

A. Immensely! I am able to calm my nerves before important matches, I am able to zone out and focus on my inner self in situations when it seems like I am alone and crowds want my opponent to win. I am able to visualise more favourable conditions than they are. For example, if they are cheering another name, I make it sound like they are cheering my name and get the energy from that. I feel that the mind is such a powerful tool and meditation helps us control it; without it, we tend to fall into a trap of fear and anxiety. That's something that I'm good at navigating past, thanks to mindfulness techniques that I'm using: breathing, singing, stillness.

Q. Why do you think it's important for young people to learn to meditate?

A. The topic of meditation is a very popular topic and young people are more and more curious about it. I find that the biggest benefit for young people who practise mindfulness is that they are enough just as they are. They don't need to seek approval and acceptance through high grades, accolades, pretending to be somebody else. They can be authentic and genuine and enjoy life listening to the inner voice that they have. Sometimes we lose connection with that inner voice because we hear others conditioning us and telling us, 'If only you do this, then ...', 'If you want this, then you MUST ...'. So we get trapped in trying to be somebody, instead of just being. The truth is we should try our best, but try not to be loved by others more or accepted by others more. We should try our best at things we love and enjoy and because we want to because we love and respect ourselves first—and luckily, by feeling whole within, we can help the world too.

Q. Do you think meditation is a superpower?

A. Definitely! And the best thing about it is we all have that superpower. Everybody is a superhero!

SUPERPOWER

HIGH HOPES

Wow! There is so much to take from Novak's advice but for the time being I want you to really think about this comment:

> 'I feel that the mind is such a powerful tool and meditation helps us control it; without it, we tend to fall into a trap of fear and anxiety.'

Such wise words! Our mind is so powerful, particularly with all those thoughts that come and go. Meditation is the tool we use to help us get better control over our thinking, our programming. Meditation can also help us overcome the fear and anxiety that we all feel from time to time. **This is why I call it a superpower.** Novak also talks about visualisation and this is another important tool that we will get to later.

Meditation is like the first step: it helps us to calm our mind and if you start meditating, you will start to think and feel differently. Be curious about how it can help you. Simply ask yourself this question: 'I wonder how meditation will help me?' Start to open yourself up to the fact that meditation can and will help you. I want you to have high hopes about what this superpower can do for you.

WHAT DO YOU HOPE MEDITATION BRINGS INTO YOUR LIFE?

HOW TO MEDITATE

Read through the instructions below and then give it a go!

Sit in a comfortable position with your eyes closed.

Start by taking a nice big breath in through your nose and then out through your mouth.

Take another nice big breath in through your nose and out through your mouth and then one more.

Now just return to your normal breath.

Just notice your breath, put all your attention onto your breathing. It might help to place your hands gently on your stomach or chest, wherever you feel your breathing the most.

Now when you breathe in, imagine that breath going all the way down to your tummy, and then let it come back out of your mouth on the exhale.

You might notice that your mind wanders off, that it doesn't want to pay attention to the breath, it wants to think about something else that happened today.

Just notice this.

Become an observer.

It's like you are just watching the thought and when you notice this thought, then bring your attention back to your breath.

Just focus on your breath.

Focus on the sensations of the breath in the body and get used to just sitting here breathing.

You might notice that your mind wants to wander off again and again.

Every time you notice this, you simply bring your attention back to your breath.

If you can stay like this for five minutes or so, you may start to notice that your body relaxes.

Just know that every time your mind wanders off and you bring it back to your breath, you are training your mind.

When you eventually open your eyes, things might feel different.

You might notice that you feel calmer or more relaxed.

Just Breathe

To download a free version of this meditation, go to greatfulness.com.au/resources and click on 'Greatfulness Library'.

KNOWING VERSUS DOING

A quick note for all of you who just skipped the meditation. Here's where you are on your journey: you are currently standing on top of the **'knowing' mountain.** Yep, that's great because you now 'know' about meditation but the real results come when you take a leap from the 'knowing' mountain to the top of the **'doing' mountain**. You are not going to get results unless you actually **do the work**. This applies to anything in your life.

IT IS THE ACTION THAT YOU TAKE EACH DAY THAT WILL HELP YOU GET TO THE NEXT LEVEL!

Sure, you can 'know' how to ride a bike. You can even watch a YouTube clip and think you know exactly how to do it, but you won't actually be able to ride a bike unless you get out there and 'do' it. **You have to take action!** You have to put in the work to get the results. At the time of writing this book, Novak Djokovic was ranked as the men's singles #1 tennis player in the world. Let me ask you something. Do you think Novak Djokovic got to be the #1 tennis player in the world because he 'knows' how to play tennis? No, he got there because he went out, day in and day out, and actually did the work, and he still does. He takes action **every single day!**

'The way to get started is to quit talking and start doing.'

— Walt Disney

FAULTY EQUIPMENT

I hope you are beginning to understand what a powerful piece of equipment your mind is. **Everything we see, think, do, feel, is first filtered through our mind.**

Now you also know that meditation is the best way to train your mind, but I want to share something else with you now that some of you might question:

 YOUR MIND CAN PLAY TRICKS ON YOU!

Yep. It's like having a faulty piece of equipment. It goes back to our 'negativity bias', our habit of usually viewing things in a negative way as opposed to a positive way. But don't just take it from me. Have a read through the bubbles below and just see where your mind goes with each scenario? **What do you tell yourself?**

1

Your friend walks past you and completely ignores you.

2

You see two of your friends whispering and laughing in the playground.

3

Your mum said she would pick you up at 3:30 and it's now 4pm and you haven't heard from her.

4

You get called to the Principal's office.

So, let me guess. In the first scenario, you have done something wrong for your friend to ignore you, and actually there is a big chance that the whole school will find out about it now and dislike you forever? In the final scenario, you are obviously being called to the

Principal's office because, yet again, you have done something wrong? I am guessing that your mind created the **worst-case scenario** for each situation rather than the **best-case scenario?** This is linked to that negativity bias that I keep going on about. So I want you to breathe a big sigh of relief, right now and just say to yourself:

PHEW! IT'S JUST MY MIND PLAYING TRICKS ON ME. THINGS AREN'T ACTUALLY ALL THAT BAD—IT'S THE WAY MY BRAIN IS HARDWIRED.

Knowledge is power, my friend, and a big part of this is simply understanding that your mind can sometimes give the wrong meaning to things. I don't want you to worry about this. I want you to take this information and use it to your advantage. We will soon get to the bit where I explain how you can make changes to ensure that your mind is helping you and not holding you back, so please hang in there. For now, all I want you to do is just recognise that this happens and perhaps think of a time when it happened to you. When did you create a worst-case scenario for yourself? If our minds are that powerful, wouldn't it be nice if we could teach ourselves how to look for the best-case scenario instead?

Go back to the scenarios on page 55.

This time, think about the best possible outcome. For example, you get called to the Principal's office because they want to congratulate you for being such an amazing student!

Or you see your friends whispering in the playground and you assume that they are planning what to get you for your birthday.

Get your imagination to work in your favour.

FEAR OF FLYING

Are you one of those people who are scared of flying? Perhaps the thought of getting onto a plane is enough to make your heart start racing? Let's talk about fear.

If you aren't scared of flying, then I want you to focus on **something that scares you.** For me, it's snakes! I am terrified of the long, slithering things. Growing up in the country did not help me overcome my fear of snakes; in fact, it kept me on high alert. I'll never forget one day when I went to ride on our motorbike and I was just about to sit on the seat when I noticed a **huge brown snake** wrapped around the handlebars. We were literally face to face. I jumped off that motorbike and ran as fast as I could back to our house. Mum was inside at the time and I **screamed** out, **'Snake!'** Within a matter of minutes, my mum had grabbed a shovel and she went down to that shed and let's just say that particular brown snake never bothered me again. **My mum is pretty tough like that!** Anyway, enough about that.

I want you to think of something that you are scared of, and just notice if you feel a sense of fear rising in your body. If you imagine the thing you fear in detail, it's likely that your body will start to have some physical response. You might notice that your heart begins to beat faster or you feel your muscles tighten. That's because your **mind doesn't actually know the difference between the real and imagined**. Your body starts to react like a real event is taking place. What's happening is that your body is going into what is known as the stress response (see page 60), and it's all to do with a certain part of our brain called the amygdala.

But before we move on, if you are feeling a little bit wobbly after imagining the very thing that you are scared of, this is a great opportunity to practise using your breathing to calm your mind and body. Take some nice deep breaths and bring yourself back to a relaxed state.

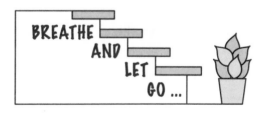

AIRPORT SECURITY

The **amygdala** isn't big, but it sure is mighty! It's about the size of an almond but it really can cause some big reactions in your body.

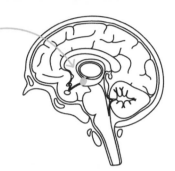

The amygdala is directly linked to survival. Its primary job is to keep you safe and out of danger. When it is activated, it causes one of three reactions:

1) fight   2) flight   3) freeze

In my scenario with Mr Brown Snake, my amygdala was activated as soon as I noticed the snake and I reacted by running away—flight, which was good instinct. Choosing to fight probably wouldn't have ended well for me!

Can you think of a time when your amygdala was activated? Perhaps you were in an argument with someone in your family? You might have gone into the fight response, and that reaction may not have led to the best outcome for you or them!

So why do you need to know about the amygdala?

Well it 'switches on' quite a bit, including when it doesn't really need to, and can cause these underlying feelings of fear. Also, when the amygdala gets switched on, it uses up a lot of energy in our body. Have you ever felt the adrenaline pumping through your body when you have been in an argument with someone? That is your stress response in action. Because of the busy world that we live in, many of us can go from one stressful situation to the next and be in a permanent state of fight, flight or freeze.

THE STRESS RESPONSE

Stress is a reaction to pressure or threat. The stress response can cause us to fight, run away, or freeze, and has an impact on the way we feel and on our nervous system.

This often means that we don't get a chance to rest our body (or our nervous system) and this can then lead to all sorts of health issues. The trick is recognising when our amygdala has been activated when it doesn't really need to be, such as sitting on the plane and feeling like your heart is about to jump out of your chest! You see, while our amygdala's job is to alert us to danger it can be a **tad overprotective!** It's a bit like airport security. You know it's their job to keep everyone safe but they sometimes walk around treating everyone with suspicion—which isn't very relaxing.

TUNING IN

GUIDING LIGHTS

Now that you recognise fear, it seems like a pretty good time to talk about some of our other feelings. You know that you have feelings but the real question is, do you know how to manage them? I am assuming that you know why they are called feelings? Because we literally **feel** them in our body.

YOUR FEELINGS ARE YOUR GUIDING LIGHTS.

When we start to pay attention to how we are feeling, it can really help to guide us.

Here are some more examples of what you might notice in your body for different feelings:

anger
clenched hands or clenched teeth

worry
a knot in your stomach or a general feeling of unease. Many children I work with say that when they worry too much, they can get a headache

nervous
butterflies in the stomach

excitement
a bit harder to describe but you most likely feel this in your stomach as well

scared
racing heart or shaking hands

love
this is a nice one to notice. You might feel a warm sensation in your heart area or just feel warm all over. It's like a glow from the inside out

61

The trick is to really stop and take notice of these feelings. Notice what your body feels like and figure out what it is trying to tell you. Are you worried about an upcoming exam? Are you angry because a friend said something mean?

When you notice that you have clenched fists, it's probably a good time to walk away and **breathe deeply.** If we can tune in and notice our feelings, we are in a much better place to do something about it. That might mean just sitting with the feelings and breathing, just to **help the feelings subside.**

SOUVENIRS

Have you ever been given a snow globe as a souvenir? They were all the rage when I was growing up! If you are not familiar with a snow globe, you give it a shake and the little flakes of 'snow' float around the ball. When you sit it back down, eventually everything settles to the bottom. **This is a great way to think about our feelings.** Something 'shakes' us up on the inside and we have all these different sensations in our body. When you notice this, give yourself permission to sit with the feelings and breathe. What you will notice is that feelings will settle back down much faster when you just allow yourself to sit with them.

Allow the feelings to be there—you can even try naming them—and then let them go.

If you pretend the feelings don't exist, this can often be harder. You can try saying:

 'Hi, Worry. I feel you in my stomach right now and I just want you to know that it's OK; we've got this.'

Once you get the hang of recognising the feelings in your body, you can become better at managing them and allowing them to subside. You can then make a choice to let them go. It might help to imagine the feeling leaving your body through your feet and returning into the earth below you.

Here are four simple ways to manage your feelings:

1. Notice the feeling: where is it, what is it, what colour is it?

2. Accept the feeling. Don't try to push it away or fight it off.

3. Feel the feeling and give it some space to be there.

4. When you feel ready, choose to let it go.

It's important to realise that our feelings are not permanent, which means that they will come and go.

If you can take the time to acknowledge your feelings and give yourself some space, you will soon become a master at dealing with the more challenging ones. If that means allowing yourself to have a good cry from time to time, go ahead! Crying can be such a good release.

Let your feelings guide you and allow yourself to feel them.

Feelings are like waves, they will come and go

TRY IT!

#practice

Has there been a time when your feelings felt too much?

Do you know what was going on in your mind and your body? The next time you start to feel a little off balance, try this simple exercise:

Sit on the floor or in a chair and close your eyes.

Take in a nice big breath, in through your nose and out through the mouth.

Then take two more nice deep breaths in through the nose and out through the mouth.

Give yourself permission to relax and take your time.

*When you feel yourself relaxing or feeling restful,
ask yourself two questions quietly in your mind:*

(1) *I notice that my mind is . . .?*

(2) *I notice that my body is . . .?*

*Simply notice what answers you come up with. Your mind
might feel busy, but your body might feel tired. Or your
mind might feel worried and your body might feel tight.*

Simply notice and allow these feelings to be there.

*Stay with your breath for as long as you can and allow the
breath to calm your mind and your body.*

Sit with the feelings and allow them to subside.

Allow everything to settle.

When you feel ready, open your eyes.

PRE-TRAVEL NERVES

It's completely normal to get nervous before a big trip.
It's also completely normal to get nervous before any
of these things:

exams   giving a presentation
meeting someone for the first time   having
difficult conversations   sports events
performances   doing something new

You might have other things that you would add to this list. Feeling nervous is just your body letting you know that there is something 'going on'. Nerves can actually be a good thing because they can give us a little bit of a 'push' to get through something that might be challenging.

The next step is to recognise how being nervous feels in your body. As we talked about earlier, many people use the saying 'butterflies in the tummy' to describe how being nervous feels. Over the years, my students have described nervous as feeling like:

knots in the tummy
feeling generally queasy and unwell
heart racing
flushed in the face

Think about a time when you were nervous. Can you remember how it actually felt? I want to let you in on a little secret: everybody gets nervous from time to time—yes, even adults! I remember I had to give a presentation a few years ago to a large group of adults (about 500 of them!). It was the first time I had ever done something like that and I literally felt sick in my stomach waiting for the moment to come around. At the same time, I really wanted to do the presentation and I knew that pushing myself out of my comfort zone was a good opportunity to grow and learn. So I did some deep breathing before I went on the stage and I tried to keep myself grounded as much as possible. And every time I felt those nerves, I would take a nice slow breath. Guess what? When I eventually got out there and did my presentation, I loved every minute of it! I was on such a high after it, as well. That feeling has encouraged me to do more in regards to stepping out of my comfort zone, but I always get nervous before I do. I've just learnt to manage the nerves and use them to my advantage.

Do you know what I say to my students about dealing with their nerves? I tell them to turn their **'butterflies'** into **dragons.** In other words, use them to give you energy and fuel. You'll soon find yourself powering through any nerve-wracking situation!

TURN YOUR BUTTERFLIES INTO DRAGONS!

Can you remember a time when you felt excited? It may have been the day before your birthday or the night before Christmas.

I want you to think back to something that made you feel really excited and see if you can remember what it feels like in your body. Your heart might have been beating faster, your stomach may have been 'buzzing' and you may have started talking faster. What you probably don't realise is that very similar things happen when you feel anxious.

!? ANXIETY AND EXCITEMENT ACTUALLY FEEL VERY SIMILAR IN OUR BODY

and this means that with practice, the next time you notice yourself getting nervous or anxious, you can reframe it as excitement instead.

I AM EXCITED!

How do you do this? The picture opposite will give you a pretty big clue.

Remember when we talked about how our minds can play tricks on us? This is one of those times when we try to take control by shifting our mindset and deliberately try to create the best possible scenario for ourselves. Simply tell yourself 'I am excited, I am excited, I am excited', and **trick your mind** and body into thinking that you are excited, instead of anxious.

Try it out. The next time you have something coming up that you know is going to challenge you, try turning the anxiety into excitement. When you can do this, there will be **no stopping you!**

The moment that you notice anxious
thoughts or feelings in your body,
choose to take three deep breaths and then
say to yourself,
'I am so excited about this (fill in the blank).
This (fill in the blank) *is really going to be fun!'*

YOUR TRAVELLING COMPANIONS

It's high time that you met your travelling companions—your trusty sidekicks who will be with you throughout your whole life journey. I'll let you in on a bit of a secret here: your travelling companions are actually characters that are inside your head.

Bear with me here! Going back to the 50,000 or more thoughts that you have on a daily basis, this actually makes up what is called our **'internal dialogue'**, which is a bit like a conversation between characters.

So, let's meet the first one:

OUR INNER CRITIC

As the name suggests, our inner critic can be pretty critical. They might be continuously judging you, the people around you and your abilities. Your inner critic might sound a bit like this:

'WHY DID YOU SAY THAT?'

'YOU CAN'T DO THAT!'

'PEOPLE ARE GOING TO LAUGH AT YOU.'

'DID YOU MAKE ANOTHER MISTAKE?'

We also have a character called:

Our inner coach

Check this guy out! Just like any good coach, the job of your inner coach is to help you become the best possible version of yourself. This also means giving you a little extra push sometimes to get you out of your comfort zone. What types of things do you think your inner coach might say?

'You've got this!'

'Why don't you give it a try, you might love it!'

'Go for it!'

'Be brave!'

We travel through our lives with both characters. The question is, **who do you listen to the most?** The voice of our inner critic can be very loud. In fact, sometimes he/she is so loud that we can't even hear the voice of our inner coach. The inner critic is closely linked to our fears, our worries and our anxiety and, just like the airport security team, wants to detect any potential threats. The inner critic is on high alert for anything that might threaten or harm you. If you look a little further at this, **you will see that the inner critic is closely linked to the amygdala.** It's probably time you got to know this character inside your head, as the inner critic can play a very important role when it comes to stopping you from trying new things.

Your inner coach, on the other hand, well, they have totally got your back. **Your inner coach wants to help you reach the next level in your life** and helps you grow and stretch yourself in different ways. Many of us shy away from being uncomfortable (because it feels uncomfortable!) but the inner coach knows that when you feel a little uncomfortable, it can be a good thing. It means that you are growing, that you are learning, and that you are pushing through in order to take your life to the next level. So, I want you to start paying attention to what your inner coach might say and when you notice the voice of your inner critic, simply reply:

'Thanks for sharing, but I am going to give this a go.'

or

'Thanks for sharing, but my inner coach and I have got this.'

WHICH WAY?

At this point in time, you are probably very keen to get going but the question is: which way?

Do you know where you are heading? My guess is that the mission makers will have a pretty good idea of which way they are heading, and the nomads might be just cruising along. It doesn't matter which type of traveller you are: having an end in mind will give you a sense of direction.

What direction do you want this adventure to go in? Considering what you have learnt so far, is there a dream or a mission or a vision that keeps coming up for you? Maybe it's too early in the journey for this to be clear and that's totally OK. If that is the case, my advice is to just keep taking the next step forward and be open to what you discover . . .

If you did come up with a clear answer, I want you now to tune in to what your inner critic might be saying about your mission? It might go something like:

'YOU CAN'T DO THAT!'

'YOU ARE NOT SMART ENOUGH OR TALENTED ENOUGH!'

'IT WILL NEVER WORK!'

So, what do you have to say to your inner critic?

'Thanks for sharing, but I am going to give this a go.'

Then tune in to your inner coach instead.

'Yay! Time to get excited!'

'Let's do this!'

'This is going to be awesome!'

This is your opportunity to tune in to excitement rather than the fear or anxiety. Remember, your inner critic will want to keep you 'safe' but ...

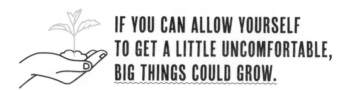

IF YOU CAN ALLOW YOURSELF TO GET A LITTLE UNCOMFORTABLE, BIG THINGS COULD GROW.

Not in the least, your confidence.

Can you think of a time in your life when you really wanted to do something but felt scared? Then eventually, maybe with the help of a trusted adult, you ended up giving that thing a go? What did it feel like once you had done it? I bet you felt like you were on top of the world! Like 'Wow, look at me go' and you were super proud of yourself. That's the feeling I want you to recognise as growth. In that moment, you have just conquered your fear and taken a step towards the, next level, you. It doesn't matter how big or small the thing was, **it's huge that you overcame the fear.**

Every time you overcome fear, you let yourself know that **you can do it**, and that is how you build confidence in yourself and take yourself to the next level.

Time to tune in to our inflight entertainment again so you can hear the amazing story of two brothers.

UP AND AWAY
with THE WRIGHT BROTHERS

Wilbur and Orville Wright were born in the late 1800s (yep, that is a while ago now!) and lived in Ohio, USA. At the young ages of eight and 11, their father brought home a foot-long helicopter device made of paper and cork and the boys became fascinated with it, sparking a deep interest in flight. As they got older, they forgot about this interest and pursued careers in publishing a weekly newspaper. Eventually, they went on to buy a sales and repair shop for bicycles, and this helped to reignite their interest in flight, and also meant that they could pay for any flying experiments they wanted to carry out. Orville and Wilbur started to gather as much information as they could about flying. They literally spent hours and hours researching from many different resources: magazines, the library and also looking at other drawings. (Remember, they didn't have any internet back then, so it took a lot longer to gather information!)

The more the brothers found out about flying, the more convinced they became that it was impossible for humans to fly, especially after another man, Otto Lilienthal, died when he attempted to fly a glider he had built. Nevertheless, the two brothers never gave up and began to pursue their dream. They tested all sorts of kites and gliders, most of which failed. In 1903, however, the brothers' perseverance finally paid off when Orville and Wilbur built The Wright Flyer. This flying 'machine' was created in their bike shop and had wooden propellers and a gasoline engine. When they first tested it, Orville's flight lasted for 12 seconds. From this point on, the sky literally was the limit!

The brothers continued to test and fly many types of planes. Their initial dream of getting man to fly in the sky had a huge impact on the world today, with planes continuing to evolve and get faster.

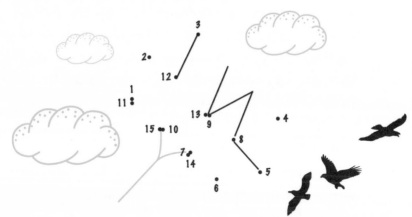

Have you ever thought about building or inventing something? Write about this in your diary. What did you try and invent and how did it go? Was there anything that you learnt from the experience?

GLOBAL CITIZEN

The Wright Brothers felt like they had a mission, and they worked hard to achieve their goal of flying a plane. They could very easily have given it all up when faced with failure after failure but they believed in their dream and thank goodness they did.

 **JUST THINK ABOUT HOW MANY PLANES FLY AROUND THE WORLD TODAY ON A DAILY BASIS!**

Planes allow us to travel to different countries quickly and relatively easily.

Planes have made this big, wide world of ours so much more accessible.

Have you been on a plane and experienced a new country? There is something pretty amazing about having the opportunity to do this, and it's probably something that many of us have taken for granted up until recently when we were told we could not travel due to COVID-19. Planes certainly help us connect to the world on a global scale. While we are talking about travelling around the globe, I think it's the perfect time to introduce you to a concept called the 'global citizen'. Have you ever heard of this before? Being a global citizen is becoming aware of the wider world and how we are all connected, then looking for ways to help other countries or citizens so that the planet can offer equal opportunities for everyone, regardless of location, race or gender.

Have you ever thought of yourself as a global citizen?

Perhaps you think you are too young to start making a difference in the life of someone else, or that there is only so much you can do in regards to helping our planet? Well, I invite you to think again. There are lots of wonderful examples of young people who are trying their best to influence change and contribute to the world in a positive way. Think about Greta Thunberg and what she has done to raise awareness about climate change. She was named *Time* magazine's Person of the Year in 2019, which is pretty amazing for any person to achieve, let alone at 16 years old!

Greta's mission has turned out to be quite a big one. I'm not saying that your mission has to be this big, but perhaps her story can inspire you to start thinking about your life in a different way.

What do you feel passionate about?

Remember, you don't have to have it all figured out: simply give yourself permission to start thinking about it.

IS THERE AN ISSUE IN THE WORLD THAT YOU WOULD LIKE TO HELP?

Examples of some current global issues

ENVIRONMENT · HEALTHCARE · CLEAN WATER · EDUCATION · EQUAL OPPORTUNITIES

Time for some more inflight entertainment!

I want to share a pretty amazing story with you now about a six-year-old who wanted to make a difference many years ago.

UP AND AWAY

with RYAN HRELJAC

When Ryan Hreljac was just six years old and sitting in his classroom in Canada, his teacher at that time, Mrs Prest, told the class that children in Africa often had to walk for hours just to get clean water. Not only that, but many children became sick or even died because they did not have access to clean water. Later, Ryan reflected:

All I had to do was take ten steps from my classroom to get to the drinking fountain and I had clean water. Before that day in school, I figured everyone lived like me. When I found out this wasn't the case, I decided I had to do something about it.

Ryan went home and spoke to his parents about it and said that he would like to try to help. So, at an age when most of us are still learning to tie our shoelaces, Ryan started doing odd jobs around the house to try to raise enough money to buy a well in Africa that would provide clean water. In four months, he had saved $70 but soon realised that he needed more like $2000 to get the well. Not one to give up easily, Ryan started speaking at Rotary clubs and slowly began to raise the money.

A YEAR OR SO LATER, RYAN HAD RAISED ENOUGH MONEY TO BUILD THE FIRST WELL IN UGANDA.

Fast-forward to now and Ryan continues to make a difference to the lives of many people living in developing countries. His original idea of helping provide clean water is now a foundation called the **Ryan's Well Foundation** and the impact it has had is pretty amazing. Since 2001, the foundation has improved the lives of over one million people in **16 different countries in Africa.** Even today, Ryan continues his work and he has raised millions of dollars to help provide clean drinking water.

PROBLEMS OR POSSIBILITIES?

ITINERARY

I hope you are now feeling a teeny bit inspired and you are ready to put together your own itinerary, which is basically a **plan for your journey.** For example, first stop Paris; second stop, London. However, the plan for this journey is really quite simple. I want you to plan for the **best-case scenario,** instead of the worst-case. **That's it!** It's quite simple when it's written down on paper, but in actual fact, it can be hard to put into practice because it takes work and your **conscious awareness.**

You now know that your mind can play tricks on you and that it can find it very easy to focus on what's going wrong. In order to combat this, we have to start making a few changes. If we want to create the best-case scenario for ourselves, we need to start thinking about what we do want, as opposed to what we don't want. How do we do this? We start by paying attention to our thoughts, which we talked about earlier. You have already done your 'inventory' and should be a bit more aware of which thoughts you might like to change. Keep those in your mind as we move into this next section, which is all about how we can start changing our thoughts to help us create the best-case scenario!

FLIGHT PATHS

Have you ever seen a flight path plotted out on the TV or somewhere else? It normally allows you to see the progress the plane is making and you also get a grasp on just how many different routes are available. It's almost like looking at a map of the sky, which is **pretty amazeballs!**

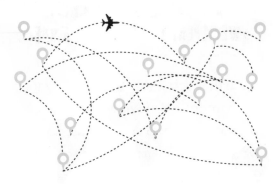

The idea of flight paths is a really good way of helping us explore **neuroplasticity.**

That's a pretty big word, hey? Try and say it like this: Nure-oh-plas-iss-it-y.

It means that our brains can literally be rewired!

Let's say that you have to fly from Sydney to London. The first time you do this trip, you are going to need to concentrate and focus on what you are doing in order to get there. You will have to plan your journey so you know what you are doing in advance, as your brain will be taking in lots of new information—you'll be creating new neural pathways as you go through each new experience.

NEURAL PATHWAYS ARE CREATED IN THE BRAIN AND BECOME STRONGER EVERY TIME WE REPEAT A THOUGHT OR A HABIT.

Now imagine that you have to fly from Sydney to London every month. You will soon be able to do this trip without having to concentrate so much because you will have a greater understanding of what you need to do—you will have already created the **neural pathway.** You'll soon be able to do this trip on autopilot.

 Let's have a look at your thoughts.

Just say you have the thought, 'I am hopeless at spelling'. With that thought, you have created a new neural pathway. Then one day, you get handed a surprise spelling test in class and you don't do very well. This will most likely confirm your thought, 'I am hopeless at spelling'. The more you think that thought, the stronger that neural pathway becomes. It's not long before this thought becomes an Automatic Negative Thought. I like to call them **ANTs:**

Automatic
Negative
Thoughts.

Without our attention, these cheeky little **ANTs** can take over and before we know it, we have a constant flow of them running through our mind: **'I'm not good enough'** or **'I need to improve'**, etc.

But the good news is that once we become aware of these **ANTs**, we can take steps to turn them into **PETs**, which stands for:

Positive
Energising
Thoughts.

Let's go back to the thought, 'I am hopeless at spelling'. This thought, of course, is not true. The REAL truth is that if you practised your spelling, you would improve. Yes, it might take some effort and work, and you might need to receive some extra help, but you could improve. So, let's turn that **ANT** into a **PET.**

Look at the table opposite, where the PET is already written in: **'If I practise my spelling, I will improve.'** Now it's your turn. Think about some of your ANTs and how you could turn them into PETs. The trick with doing this is to make the PETs realistic for you—make sure it is something that you **believe is achievable** for you. If you set a goal that you know is completely out of your reach for the time being, it could lead to further disappointment.

Another example might help. Say that you have a swimming carnival coming up at school. You recognise that you have an ANT regarding your swimming skills: 'I am such a bad swimmer, I know I will come last in my race' and you decide that you would like to turn this ANT into a PET. Remember to keep your PET realistic. An unrealistic PET would be something along the lines of, 'I'm going to practise so much that I will set a new school record'. Because, deep down, you already know that it's unlikely that you will remain committed to that goal. A more realistic goal (or PET) would be: 'I am going to start practising and really give it my best shot to improve my skills and confidence.'

 **BY WORKING ON YOUR SKILLS, YOU WILL GAIN MORE CONFIDENCE AND WHEN YOU FEEL MORE CONFIDENT, GUESS WHAT? YOU ARE MORE LIKELY TO SWIM YOUR BEST!**

ANT

'I am hopeless at spelling'

PET

'If I practise my spelling, I will improve'

You might like to draw up a similar table in your diary. This is your chance to have a think about how you can change those Automatic Negative Thoughts into something more positive and energising.

AUTOPILOT

An **automatic pilot** is a device that is used during a flight to make a plane fly without the pilot. Can you think of a time that you have been on autopilot? Have you ever done something without really thinking about it too much?

AUTOMATIC PILOT *(noun)*

a device for keeping an aircraft on a set course without the intervention of the pilot

Maybe some of these activities:

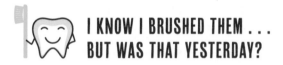

eating ✈ brushing teeth or hair
getting dressed ✈ riding in the car
talking ✈ thinking ✈ reading

We can all do activities without really paying attention to what we are doing. For example, you might get dressed one morning and put your jumper on backwards because you are not really thinking about what you are doing, or your mum or dad might ask you if you have brushed your teeth and you have to really think about it because you can't actually remember.

I KNOW I BRUSHED THEM . . . BUT WAS THAT YESTERDAY?

Being on autopilot can help us to do things without using too much energy. This is good because it means that we can save our energy for the bigger things we need to focus on. However, if we go through our entire lives on autopilot, then it might feel a bit … 'meh!' We might begin to wonder where all the adventure has gone because we feel like we are just

'going through the motions'.

Now, here's something interesting. As you already know, **approximately 90% of what we think about today are the same thoughts as we had yesterday.** Yep, you read that right: 90%! It's like getting up each morning and turning on the same playlist **every single day.** Then we go through our day, listening to the same songs over and over again and **it never really occurs to us that we could stop the playlist.** Better yet, we can create a brand-new playlist. Yes, this might take a little bit of time but wouldn't you go ahead and do it if you knew it was going to result in a much brighter, happier and more exciting playlist?

 ## IMAGINE THE POSSIBILITIES AVAILABLE TO YOU IF THE PLAYLIST OF YOUR THOUGHTS WAS A BIT MORE UPLIFTING?

If it was a playlist that made you feel good, despite what was going on around you? That doesn't mean that you need to delete every sad or negative thought, because they will always come and go. But remember you can always choose to put on a new song (or have a new thought), if and when you want to.

 ## You are in charge of what you are listening to.

CHOOSING YOUR PLAYLIST

There are really no rules when it comes to creating a new playlist. **The only limit is your imagination.** You could choose any artist, from any time, in any style. If you have ever created your own playlist, you might know that it can be lots of fun and it can make you feel good.

Or does it?

I have seen many people who choose to create a playlist that makes them feel quite sad or lonely. Others fill theirs with songs that can make them feel angry or agitated.

 THINK ABOUT WHAT SONGS YOU ARE ADDING TO YOUR PLAYLIST.

Ultimately, you want to choose the music that lifts you up, makes you feel good and gives you hope for a better future. Start becoming conscious of what you are listening to. Yes, sometimes listening to a sad song can help us better connect to what we are feeling on the inside. Or listening to an angry song might help us connect to something that we are angry about. There is nothing wrong with this! Music is really powerful in helping us connect with the way we are feeling. What I am asking you to do is to **start paying attention** to the music you are drawn to. Do you often listen to sad songs, or do you listen to lyrics that make you feel agitated or hostile?

Then just ask yourself:

 'Does this make me feel good?'

Music literally has the power to shift your energy and it can also add a new level of intensity to how you are feeling, so choose to move your energy in a positive way when you can. Remember, it's good to feel healthy and happy, and by choosing the right playlist, music really can give you a boost when you need it. Or simply try this: the next time you are feeling sad, play one of your 'happy' songs. A song that you know makes you feel good and just see what happens!

Grab your diary now and write down your ultimate playlist. Remember to include all those songs that make you feel happy and healthy. If you can, I recommend actually creating that playlist for yourself and put it on the next time you need a bit of a boost!

UNLIMITED POSSIBILITIES

I encourage you to reflect on your general view of how life is meant to be. Are you open to **new possibilities** and **new ways of being** or are the doors firmly shut due to fear of failing?

 ## WHAT DO YOU BELIEVE IS POSSIBLE FOR YOU?

Let's revisit our thoughts, feelings, behaviour triangle to help us here.

thoughts

behaviour   feelings

If your answer is **'I can achieve anything I want'**, then you may be **feeling** excited, perhaps a little pumped to get started and ready to take action (which would be your behaviour). But if your answer is **'I am limited in what I can achieve'**, you may be **feeling** wary (even resentful) and not really sure that you should take any action. Whatever the answer is for you, I want to remind you of a couple of things before we move on to the next leg of journey.

1. You are exactly where you are meant to be.

2. You are worthy of happiness and success.

3. Give yourself permission to dream.

4. The world REALLY is full of unlimited possibilities.

5. Open the door and see what else is possible for you.

PART TWO:
ON YOUR WAY!

TRUST YOURSELF

Your bags are packed. Is your passport ready?

MORE IMPORTANTLY, DO YOU FEEL LIKE YOU ARE READY TO TAKE YOUR LIFE TO THE NEXT LEVEL?

If your answer is 'not really', then you are doing fine. As any good explorer will tell you, sometimes you've just got to start and see what happens next. A big part of your journey is learning as you go and accepting that you **might never feel 100% ready.** The trick really is to have an end in mind and then just keep taking **one step forward every day until you get there**. Even if you don't have an end in mind, don't worry! Just keep moving forward and you never know where it might lead you.

To help us get into the second part of our journey together, I want to share some more inflight entertainment with you. This is an amazing story of a young person who literally just kept taking the next step ...

> Just keep taking the next step, that's all you need to do.

UP AND AWAY

with Isaiah Dawe

Today, at age 23, Isaiah Dawe is the Founder and Chief Executive Officer of a not-for-profit organisation called **ID. Know Yourself.** This charity helps young Indigenous people who are, for many different reasons, not able to live at home with their own family and are put into foster care. Isaiah's own experience in the foster care system moved him to do something to help others. By the time he was 18 years old, Isaiah had lived with 17 different foster families, and most of these were non-Indigenous, which made it very difficult for him to stay connected to his Butchulla and Gawara roots. For Isaiah, those years were very challenging, and the experience had a very negative impact on him and his self-confidence.

Thankfully, one day Isaiah met a man by the name of Eric Bell who was a Ngunnawal Elder and a valued member of the Indigenous community. Eric taught Isaiah many things but most importantly he taught him how to **respect himself** and he reconnected him with his family and culture. It was through this reconnection that Isaiah decided that he also wanted to contribute to his community in a positive and meaningful way, and since then he has worked extremely hard to build and grow ID. Know Yourself.

At any time, Isaiah could have chosen differently. He could have allowed the difficulty he'd experienced, and the anger and the negativity he felt from that, to stop him. Instead, with the help of Eric and others, and his connection to his history, he stayed strong and pushed through. Isaiah was brave when faced with adversity and met each challenge put before him. He literally just kept taking the next right step for him. He wasn't always sure where the journey was going to take him, but he came to understand the **power of his choices** and wanted to help others embrace this power themselves. Isaiah says:

Most young Indigenous people in care don't have a choice. They are stripped of their community, culture, identity, and belonging. Statistics show they will not finish high school, become homeless, and end up in the criminal justice system. They have no choices. But at ID. Know Yourself, we give them choice. Choice that enables them to become whoever they want to be, to show them that it doesn't matter where you come from in life, it's where you are going that truly matters. That you can't change the past, but how you react to it reflects your future.

The power of possibility is incredible and reminding yourself that anything is achievable despite your circumstances or situations in life is tremendously valuable. I have always envisioned a life beyond my circumstances. I would have never imagined the opportunities that I have been able to grasp over the last couple of years. From a young boy, who couldn't read or write, who had to repeat Year 4, and who couldn't even write his name. But after keeping the mindset that anything is possible and believing in myself when most people didn't, I became the first Aboriginal person awarded the TAFE NSW Student Graduate of the Year in 2017, I was the first Aboriginal person to be appointed chair of the NSW Youth Advisory Committee, Finalist for the 2019 Channel 7 Young Achiever Award and I was even a part of the First Indigenous team to sail in the prestigious Sydney to Hobart Yacht race!

By envisioning a life beyond your circumstances, knowing it is possible and believing in yourself, your dreams are achievable too.'

'The power of possibility is incredible.'
— Isaiah Dawe

Imagine yourself filling with courage; from your head to your toes!
Now ask yourself: What is the next right step I could take today?

WHICH WAY?

DEPARTURE DAY

You've made all the plans and now the big day has arrived and you are heading to the airport. This is the day that you have been waiting for.

Or is it?

Because, if the truth be told, when you are on the way to the airport, you may notice that you feel a little bit anxious. You may hear the voice of your inner critic getting a little bit louder:

'This is not going to work!' or **'What if something bad happens?'**

But ... BAM! You remember that you have prepared for this and you now understand what is happening. **Thank that amygdala of yours for trying to keep you safe!** Then take a big breath, close your eyes and tune in to your inner coach instead. What does your inner coach have to say?

'It's going to be OK.'

So you make a choice to tune into the excitement instead—literally give yourself permission to get excited. You reflect on the fact that you are about to embark on the greatest adventure of your life!

Allow yourself to be lifted by that feeling and soak in it. You may not have it all figured out, but that's totally OK. You are hopefully beginning to understand that not knowing is actually part of the fun! Rather than creating the worst-case scenario for yourself, you are now being guided by the question:

WHAT IS THE NEXT BEST STEP FOR ME?

THE POWER OF CHOICE

Remember in the last section when I said, **'You make a CHOICE to tune in to the excitement instead'**? This is actually a really important point.

We are constantly making choices.

What did you choose for breakfast this morning?

Did you choose to be kind today or not so kind?

Did you make a choice to listen or not listen?

Whether we are aware of our choices or not, they will all have an **impact on our future.** Say, for example, I made a choice today that I was going to eat fast food for every meal over the next six months. How is my future looking? It could be looking pretty unhealthy, right? So what if instead I made the choice to eat healthy foods, how would my future look then? It would be looking much better!

What many of us don't realise is that a big part of taking our life to the next level is becoming aware of what **we are choosing to do in this very moment.**

You might say that most things are chosen for you right now, like having to wear a uniform to school. Decisions like this are usually made to try to make life easier for you, even if it may not feel like that! Imagine how long it would take you to get ready in the morning if you had to choose an outfit every day? But even with something like a school uniform, you can still choose to wear it, or not. **Maybe you have chosen not to wear it one day. How did that work out?** It's important to realise that

ALL OUR CHOICES HAVE CONSEQUENCES

or end results. Sometimes the end results will be great and at other times, perhaps not so great. When the results aren't great, that is the perfect opportunity to ask yourself:

 'OK, what did I learn?'

Sometimes we make decisions that can have a bigger impact. Let's go back to the story of Isaiah Dawe. Isaiah came to understand the power of his choices and their potential impact on others, and he decided to use this knowledge to his advantage. He now helps other young people recognise this simple, but powerful piece of information.

CAN YOU SEE HOW OUR CHOICES HAVE A RIPPLE EFFECT?

That is, when we make a choice it has an impact on everyone around us.

 **When have you made a really good choice?** How did it affect those around you?

SETTING YOUR GPS

 IF YOU DO NOT KNOW WHERE YOU ARE GOING, EVERY ROAD WILL GET YOU NOWHERE.
— HENRY A. KISSINGER

Let's say that your parents decide to take you on a family holiday. The first thing you would probably ask is, **'Where are we going?'** What if they turned around and said to you, **'We have no idea, we are just going to start driving and see what happens'**? Would that make sense to you? It might sound like a **'crazy adventure'** but can you imagine when you get to the very first roundabout and Mum says, **'Turn right**' and Dad says, **'No, I want to keep going straight'**? This 'crazy adventure' might quickly turn into plain old **'crazy'**, with everyone demanding to go home after an hour of arguments and driving around in circles!

 It helps to have an idea of where you are going.

If you can point yourself in the general direction of where you would like to go, or what you would like to achieve, it really can make your life's journey much smoother. It will also help you when it comes to making choices, because you can always ask yourself, **'Is this where I want to be going?'** Let's look at an example.

Say you have a dream of becoming a professional sportsperson. That's great! You have an end goal, or general direction, in mind.

IT'S LIKE YOU HAVE PUT A DESTINATION INTO YOUR PERSONAL GPS.

Now you can start taking steps towards this goal every single day and these steps will be made up of the decisions that you make. So yes, that bag of lollies might look tempting but is eating that bag of lollies going to support your goal of becoming a professional sports player? Or, say you get asked to a friend's sleepover party on the same day that you are meant to be playing in a tournament. Yes, it's a hard decision to have to make, but what is more important in the long run? What supports the direction you want to be going in?

A little while ago, **Chloe Logarzo** visited my children's school to talk about her soccer career playing as a midfielder for the **Matildas.** My daughter loves soccer so she was very excited to hear Chloe talk. When she got home from school,

I asked her how it all went and she said to me,

'Mum, she talked about how hard she has to train and how that meant she missed out on lots of birthday parties when she was growing up!'

This piece of information really stayed with my daughter. Listening to Chloe talk made her realise that when you choose to do something like play professional sports, it's not a straightforward journey.

You are going to have to make **choices** every day that support your dream. Even choosing to get the right amount of sleep so you are on top of your game is something that you will need to consider.

Can you see now that when you have a direction in mind, it can really help guide your choices?

HEADVENTURE

It's time now to introduce you to an exciting new tool that can help you immensely on your journey. I call it having a Headventure, but you might also like to refer to it as visualisation or 'mental rehearsal'.

 **IT'S THE PROCESS WHERE WE USE OUR MINDS TO START PICTURING WHAT WE WOULD LIKE TO CREATE IN OUR FUTURE.**

We literally start imagining an outcome that we would like to see happen. This process can really help us when it comes to creating the best-case scenario for ourselves. Professional athletes have been using visualisation for years. Remember our first inflight entertainment episode with Novak? Let me remind you what he said about visualisation:

I listened to music, I visualised lifting trophies and being the #1 tennis player in the world. I was practising my victory speeches and making trophies out of card boxes. I think it brought good energy and vibes to what I was doing.

Pretty cool, hey? Novak rehearsed (mentally and physically) becoming the #1 tennis player in the world.

He started creating pictures in his mind and this has helped him achieve his goals. So how does it work?

Well, it's quite fascinating that most human minds tend to think in pictures.

I want you to try something that should help you 'see' this.

Find a comfortable spot and close your eyes. When you have your eyes closed, focus on your breathing and get yourself into a relaxed state.

Then I want you to think of the following things:

someone
you love

your
house

your
school

your
favourite
food

What happened? It's likely that when you thought of these things, you saw a picture. It's like an image or snapshot flashes into your mind. If you close your eyes again (you can do it now!) all you will notice is black. You know the best thing about this black is that you can use it as your very own movie screen. You can literally start making your own 'mind movies'.

Now give this little practice a go. Just have a play around with it and see what happens.

Close your eyes and take some nice deep breaths to get relaxed.

Now I want you to picture in your mind a place that you have always wanted to visit.

It can be anywhere in the world.

Where would you like to be? Picture that place in detail.

Notice the tourist attractions that you would like to see or if there is a nice place in nature that you would like to go and sit.

What is it about that place that you want to see and experience?

Try to imagine it now in as much detail as you can.

Give yourself permission to explore it all!

When you feel like you have finished exploring, open your eyes.

Well done! How did that feel? Don't worry if you weren't able to do it, it just takes a little bit more practice for some people. Or you might have noticed that something else came up for you? Maybe you could 'feel' things rather than 'see' them.

There is no right or wrong way to do this. Some people will be able to use mental imagery a lot easier than others. At this stage, it's more about growing your awareness that this **can** be done and just have a play around with it. Treat it as a bit of fun and don't worry if you can't do it yet. I like to call it Headventure because it's literally like taking an adventure in your head. The best way to make use of this is to start picturing scenarios that you would like to see happen.

To help you better understand how visualisation can help, I think it's time for some more inflight entertainment.

This time we will hear from Dr Doty, who is a Professor at Stanford University. Dr Doty hasn't always had any easy life—things were actually pretty chaotic for him growing up—but thankfully, when he was about ten, he met a lovely lady called Ruth who changed his life forever by introducing him to two magic tricks ...

UP AND AWAY
with DR DOTY

Q. Ruth taught you two magic 'tricks'. The first one was meditation and the second one was visualisation. Can you explain the difference between the two?

A. Meditation allows you to calm the mind and be present while visualisation allows you to manifest your intentions.

Q. Did you ever think that your visualisation of becoming a neurosurgeon wasn't going to work?

A. I believe doubt is common especially when you start but I found that the more I visualised my intentions, the more likely they were to manifest.

Q. How has meditation helped you over the years?

A. Meditation has resulted in me being more relaxed and being more present which results in the executive control areas in the front of your brain to function at their best allowing for more thoughtful decision-making, more creativity and more productivity. This results also in being able to connect better with people and understand their perspective and be more compassionate.

Q. How do you think your life would be different now if you had not met Ruth and started using meditation and visualisation?

A. I'm very appreciative of what Ruth gave me in terms of her time and her training my mind. Some would argue that based on my personality structure, I would have succeeded regardless. Of course, we will never know. Each of us has to deal with the situation we are given. Speculation of what might have been or could have been can be destructive.

Q. What is the one piece of advice you have for a young person starting out with these tools?

A. The greatest challenge is being patient. Especially when you are young, you want results immediately but there is no endeavour worth having that does not require patience and effort. So stick with it.

Q. Do you think meditation and visualisation are superpowers?

A. Absolutely. And they are available to everyone for free. One simply has to make the effort and be patient.

'There is no endeavour worth having
that does not require patience and effort.'

— Dr Doty

ACTION!

TALES FROM ABROAD

Dr Doty's story is a great example of how meditation and visualisation can help you. I could share lots of research with you about how meditation works, but I figure that you would probably be more interested in hearing stories from real people. **Because you know what?** When you start to realise how these tools have helped other people, you start to see the possibilities for your own life.

Would you like to know a few more people who use meditation and/or visualisation?

Katy Perry ⭐ Michael Jordan
Michael Phelps ⭐ Hugh Jackman
Lady Gaga ⭐ Usher ⭐ Oprah

That's just to name a few! There are literally hundreds of examples of well-known people who use these tools, and there are millions of not so well-known people as well. I know for me personally, meditation has helped in so many ways.

When I experienced depression, to be totally honest, I didn't think I would ever feel normal again. However, one day a doctor recommended meditation to me and I totally believed that it wouldn't work, but I was willing to try anything in order to feel good again. I started quite slowly (five to ten minutes a day) and then built up to about 20 minutes a day. Now I meditate at least once a day and it's a huge part of my life. When I say, 'It has helped me in so many ways', what I mean is, it:

- ✓ improves my sleep
- ✓ decreases my levels of stress and anxiety
- ✓ improves my mood
- ✓ helps me deal with challenging thoughts and feelings
- ✓ improves my relationships
- ✓ helps my confidence
- ✓ makes me generally happier.

In all honesty, I can say that it **has literally changed my life!** I cannot imagine where I would be without it. It's actually what motivates me to teach it now, because I really am living proof that this 'stuff' works, and that's why I want to share it with you.

If you are sitting there thinking, **'It's not going to work for me'**, that's exactly what I thought too! I beg you to just try it and see what happens. But remember, like anything, it's going to require you to do some work. You are literally going to have to …

PUT DOWN YOUR DEVICES AND ANY OTHER DISTRACTIONS AND CHOOSE TO CONNECT WITH YOURSELF INSTEAD.

MEDITATION IS TAKING THE TIME TO TURN OUR ATTENTION TO THE INSIDE.

I hope I've made you curious! Here's another simple visualisation practice. Go on, give it a go.

Start by closing your eyes and taking three deep breaths.

Give yourself permission to relax and just stay with each breath, one after the next. Allow the breath to relax you.

Stay with your breathing until you feel like you are at a neutral point; not excited, agitated or frustrated, just relaxed.

Now, picture in your mind's eye that you are sitting inside a plane and you're just about to take off. You are not quite sure where you are going, but you know it will be somewhere special. The plane lifts high into the sky and you are buzzing with excitement.

You look out the window and see your hometown disappearing into the distance.

You relax into your seat, feeling very safe and secure and you allow your mind to drift.

A voice comes over the loudspeaker, asking you to prepare for landing.

When you arrive, it's like you have landed at some place in the future.

You look around and it's like you have landed in your own special time and place!

You start to understand that this is your life in ten years' time.

As you look around, you notice that everything is about you, but in the future.

You notice photographs of yourself.

What do you look like in ten years' time?

You see awards and certificates hanging on a wall.

What are they for?

Take a moment now to recognise what you have achieved in ten years.

What else do you see? Perhaps you can see pictures of loved ones or people who are important in your life.

Notice what you are doing in ten years' time. What do you do for your career and how might you be contributing to the world?

Just have a look around now and take it all in.
This is your special place.

This is the future you.

Then you hear the voice over the loudspeaker again, asking you to get back on the plane, because it's time for you to head back.

You climb onboard and you are filled with wonder and awe.

You feel calm but excited by what you saw.

You take a moment to reconnect with your breath and bring your senses back into your physical body. You might like to wiggle your fingers and toes and then when you are ready, open your eyes.

THE PLACES YOU'LL DISCOVER

With visualisation, there are so many places you can discover! This is where your imagination can be your **best friend.** It's here that we start to use our imagination for good rather than creating the worst outcome. Visualising is a bit like daydreaming, but instead of being by accident, it's something that you do on purpose. I want to talk about this for a little bit because it's actually really important. What is the difference between daydreaming and visualisation?

 ## THE KEY IS TAKING ACTION!

Any one of us can lie on the couch and daydream, but that's when it quite literally stays as a dream inside your head.

 The key to making that dream a reality is to imagine it (on the movie screen in your mind) and then take action.

Let's use this book as an example. Yes, I have dreamed about writing a book (I have wanted to be a writer since I was a young girl but that's another story!) and yes, I have visualised this book for the past

18 months at least (probably longer by the time this book is in your hands) but guess what?

There would be no book if I didn't sit down to write it. I literally had to get up every morning and set aside time to write. When I was busy teaching, I still had to try to find the time to take action on this book and I did that because I was **committed to my dream of writing this book.**

Novak Djokovic's tennis career is no different. He had a dream to be the #1 tennis player in the world and had to take action every day to achieve it.

 SO PLEASE, GO AHEAD AND DREAM AWAY.

Allow your mind to open up and imagine yourself taking your life to the next level. Then sit down and work out what it's going to take for you to reach that dream.

 What action do you need to take?

Be honest with yourself: how committed are you to reaching that dream? If you feel 100% committed (willing to give it everything and make sacrifices in order to achieve it), then good for you, you are certainly heading down the right track!

BOARDING PASS

Having a dream or a vision in mind is like choosing a destination, which we talked about earlier. You give yourself permission to head in a certain direction, and that's a good thing. Yes, you might get 'off course' and it might not all go as planned but remember that is all part of the journey.

Have you ever been given a boarding pass for a plane? It's a pretty exciting moment. It's like you finally have permission to get on board the plane and travel to your new destination. It can be a life-changing moment because you know you are about to embark on something new. There is still lots to learn but you know what general direction you are going in.

But what if you don't know what direction you should go in? What do you do in that situation? Well, the answer is to take the next step in front of you and see where that leads. Ask yourself, **'What is the next step that feels right?'** It comes back to the power of our choices, remember? Every single day is filled with choices. If you don't have the 'big picture' figured out, you start by making the best choice available to you in that moment, but this means that you have to be aware and pay attention. One of the greatest things you can do is become aware when you have a choice to make.

You can simply ask yourself:

'IS THIS A GOOD CHOICE
FOR ME RIGHT NOW?'

What is 'right now'?

The fastest way to bring your attention to 'right now' is to tune into your breath. Your breath can only ever be in the present moment so simply choose to take three deep breaths and connect to your body. When we are in the 'now' moment, we can tune into what actually feels 'right' for us.

Practise with a question like, 'Is playing my iPad the best next step for me right now or is there something else I could do with my time?' and see what answers come up. You might feel guided to go outside and play instead and when you do this, you might realise how good it feels. This is about really listening to what we need, from the inside out, and being open to doing things in a new way.

It seems like such a simple thing, but when was the last time you stopped and asked yourself, 'What do I choose right now?' The answer might surprise you.

ONWARDS AND UPWARDS

Most people want their general direction in life to head in an 'upwards' direction, but it can be hard. We all make mistakes and meet challenges along the way. Don't beat yourself up if you make a mistake— we are human and that means that we are not perfect. I want you to remember that it's **totally OK to make a mistake.** Maybe you would like to check in with an adult you trust on this one? I am sure that they will be the first to tell you that, yes, they have made mistakes and, yes, they have experienced failure and disappointments.

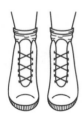 **A BIG PART OF BEING AN ADVENTURER IS ACCEPTING THAT YOU MIGHT HAVE TO TAKE SOME DETOURS OR DEAL WITH DISAPPOINTMENT ALONG THE WAY.**

Say for example you have planned to climb Mount Awesome, but due to snow, you are forced to climb Mount Average instead. The question is, what did climbing Mount Average teach you? My bet is that you have an additional bag full of lessons and experiences from that little detour. Perhaps you had to climb Mount Average to help prepare you for Mount Awesome?

A mistake or detour doesn't mean that your event or dream won't happen; it just might happen in a different way to what you originally had planned. It can be helpful to view any detours as preparation—the preparation that you may have needed without even realising you needed it! Having said all of that, I do hope you are beginning to realise that there is nothing wrong with aiming high. By all means, **reach for the stars** ... but also be willing to accept any detours along the way.

Reach for the stars – you might just catch one!

COMING THROUGH

THE F-WORDS

The dreaded F-words: **'fear'** and **'failure'**! Let's spend a little bit more time talking about these all-important F-words because they can be so scary for many of us and can have a huge impact on our life.

We have already spoken about fear and how this impacts our bodies (refer back to page 58 if you need a reminder), so it seems like a good time to bring this all together—literally.

Let's combine our two F-words to make a new statement that you may already be familiar with:

 **FEAR OF FAILING!**

Have you ever been in class and really wanted to contribute to a group discussion but you didn't because you thought you might get it wrong (and that people would laugh)? OR, have you ever been asked to try something new and then did your best to get out of it, because you thought you would mess it up in front of other people?

You are not alone when it comes to having a fear of failing. **We have all felt like this from time to time.**

Yep, even us big kids (oops, I mean adults!). First of all, I want you to understand how common this fear is and second, I want you to know that you can overcome it simply by choosing to look at it in a different way.

Wouldn't it be great if we could share our 'epic fails' openly so we could learn from each other, rather than feel like we shouldn't leave the house just in case we make a mistake? When I teach Greatfulness, I actually encourage my students to do exactly that. We set up an area in their classroom and put the heading:

FAILURE = FEEDBACK

Each time a student 'fails', they write it on a post-it note and share what they learnt. At the end of the day that's all failure is: feedback.

Have you heard of **Thomas Edison?** He was an inventor and is known for his part in inventing the first incandescent light bulb in 1879. Many scientists and inventors had been trying for years to invent artificial light and Edison was the first to create a bulb that could be easily reproduced. He failed many times when trying to invent the light bulb but took the view that failure was just feedback. There are a lot of different views on exactly how many times he tried and failed, some in the 10,000s!

We may never know how many times it didn't work, but the important thing here is that he persisted despite the failures.

CAN YOU IMAGINE PERSISTING WITH SOMETHING FOR A LONG TIME BEFORE YOU ACTUALLY SUCCEEDED?

It takes an enormous amount of courage and determination. In fact, it's pretty remarkable to keep going when all you experience is failure.

The moral of the story? Just try! It really doesn't matter if you fail.

We all fail from time to time. It's what you can learn from the failure that's most important.

Can you think about a time when you failed? How did it feel and more importantly what did you learn?

EMERGENCY FIRST AID

Are you beginning to see how much of an impact fear can have on your life?

Fear can be associated with worry, as this definition explains:

TO THINK ABOUT PROBLEMS OR UNPLEASANT THINGS THAT MIGHT HAPPEN IN A WAY THAT MAKES YOU FEEL UNHAPPY AND FRIGHTENED.

— CAMBRIDGE ENGLISH DICTIONARY

I am sure that you have already experienced worry in your life. **Most of us have sat around thinking about problems or unpleasant things that might happen.** In fact, some of us can be pretty darn good at it! What's even more interesting is that:

we can spend a great deal of time worrying about things that never happen.

Researchers found that 85% of what we worry about never happens. **Can you believe that?** Many of us spend a lot of time worrying about things in an attempt to try to control or figure out a situation or problem. The truth is that this worry never gets us anywhere.

Worry is like a rocking chair. It gives you something to do but doesn't get you anywhere.

The all-important question is, **what can we do about it?**

The first step is to notice when you are caught up in a cycle of worrying thoughts. Remember our thoughts, feelings, behaviour triangle? You might notice that you are feeling knots in your stomach and that your body is trying to tell you that you are worried. Ask yourself: is there something that I am worrying about?

I am guessing that at some time, someone has said to you, 'Don't worry.' If only it was this easy! It's like saying to someone, 'You need to calm down' when you see that they are clearly upset or frustrated. It just doesn't help.

If you have ever experienced worry, then you know it can feel pretty horrible, so I want to show you how to set up your own Emergency First Aid for dealing with worry. Or maybe a better way of doing this is for you to create your own bag of tricks for conquering worry.

BAG OF TRICKS!

If you've watched the movie Mary Poppins then you would know that she had an amazing bag of tricks. The things she could pull out of that bag of hers were simply **extraordinary.** Who knew exactly what was in that bag! What you really needed to help you make sense of Mary's 'bag of tricks' was a good imagination. Let's use our imaginations now and create our own tools for your own amazing bag of tricks.

1) **PAUSE BUTTON.** I want you to start thinking about your breath as a powerful pause button. Every time you take a breath, you hit pause on your nervous system. Inhale slowly and deeply through your nose and try to keep your shoulders relaxed. Imagine that breath going right down into your belly, and even pushing your belly out like a balloon. Exhale slowly through your mouth and repeat this for a few minutes until you sense that things have slowed down.

2) **THREE DEEP BREATHS.** When you stop and connect to your breath, you are immediately giving yourself permission to slow down. You are actually calming your nervous system by focusing on your breath. Give it a try now. Take three deep breaths and see how you feel.

If you still feel agitated or worried when you open your eyes, try to stay there for a bit longer until you get to a place of calm, when everything feels comfortable again.

3) **MEDITATION.** This is obviously connected to our breathing, as we often focus on the breath during a meditation practice. What meditation does, however, is build up your ability to cope with worry. Let's say you have done six months of meditation ahead of an exam. That practice will help you manage any worry that comes up. In fact, you might even go into that exam feeling completely 'neutral' about it. Wouldn't that be nice? Meditation is a tool that we can start doing now and it will help us in the long term. It builds our mental fitness.

4) **TALK IT OUT.** Is there someone close to you that you can talk to, someone you trust? It's usually better to choose someone who is older than you (like Mum or Dad) because quite often they will have experienced worry and know how to help. Sometimes, all we need to do is **TALK** our worries through with someone, and by just sharing them, it can help get them out of our minds. Worry can often feel much worse when we are trying to deal with it on our own. Remember, that sometimes our minds can play

tricks on us and create thoughts that are not really helpful. By sharing these thoughts with an adult, it can help us to make sense of what is fact and what is fiction.

5 **WRITE IT DOWN.** If you don't want to talk, you could create a time and space to write your worries down on paper. This process helps you get them out of your head. There has been many a time when I have helped someone write their worries down on paper only for them to look at what they have written and say, 'Why was I so worried about that?'

If you prefer drawing to writing, you might even want to try drawing your worries. What do they look like, what colour are they? You might even decide to come up with a name for each different worry that you have drawn.

6 **MOVE YOUR BODY.** Other times, it is worth getting up and moving your body. If you recognise that you are stuck in a cycle of worrying thoughts, go for a quick walk, or take your shoes and socks off and do 20 star jumps on the grass. Try to do something that will shift your energy (and thoughts) in a different direction. This is also where you could try choosing an uplifting song from your playlist. See if the music can help shift your thinking.

7 **LET IT GO.** Remember: our thoughts are not facts. Give yourself permission to let the worrying thought go. You might like to visualise yourself writing that worry onto a leaf, placing it into a river and waving it goodbye. Or you could picture it as a cloud in the sky that gently drifts off into the distance.

PAUSE BUTTON   THREE DEEP BREATHS

MOVE YOUR BODY   BAG OF TRICKS!   MEDITATION

LET IT GO   TALK IT OUT

WRITE IT DOWN

Can you think of anything else that you might like to pack?

There are no rules when it comes to using the tools in your bag of tricks. Start with the tool that you think will help you. If that doesn't work you can always try something else.

Go to your diary and write down your own bag of tricks. Include the items mentioned above but also have a think about what types of other things you would like to add. Is there anything else that you know helps you when you feel worried?

TURBULENCE

LADIES AND GENTLEMEN, THE CAPTAIN HAS TURNED ON THE 'FASTEN SEATBELT' SIGN. WE ARE NOW ENCOUNTERING SOME TURBULENCE. PLEASE RETURN TO YOUR SEATS AND KEEP YOUR SEATBELTS FASTENED. THANK YOU.

In every journey, there will be moments of turbulence.

If you have ever experienced turbulence on a plane, you'll know what I mean when I say that things may get a little bumpy! You can be flying along nice and smoothly and then all of sudden the **seatbelt sign goes on** and things can start to get a little bit shaky.

When this happens, it's a good time to sit down and start taking some **deep breaths**. You may sense that fear is sitting right next to you (as your amygdala starts to activate) but you can still choose to breathe your way through it.

Everyone experiences turbulence. All of us face challenges at some point in time. It might be a small challenge, like an exam (which can feel huge at the time), or it might be a more serious challenge, like the COVID-19 pandemic. At times like these, we can really feel knocked down and unsure of what to do next. It might even make you want to question things, particularly:

I often get asked this question when I am teaching, and because there really are no straightforward answers, I share a poem instead:

WHY?

There is a reason for everything
some people may say,
and when bad things happen
you should kneel down and pray.

But others want more
the answers aren't clear,
for when bad things happen
we can live with great fear.

When people are hurting
through no fault of their own,
or some tragedy happens
in the town where you've grown.

There are no easy answers
to the question of why,
no soft landing
when we fall down and cry.

In this world that we live in
we can't always be sure
that we'll escape the challenges;
that we won't trip and fall.

No night without day
no joy without sad,
no love without hate
and no good without bad.

When bad things do happen
beyond your control,
be kind to yourself;
make that your main goal.

Look for the good
and feel the support
of the people around you;
make them your resort.

And just like the waves
that ebb and flow in the sea,
know that things will soon change
and one day you'll be free.

UNEXPECTED DETOURS

It's worth noting that every so often something big might happen that can stop our travel adventures in their tracks. It might be something on a personal level, such as the loss of a loved one, or it could be something on a global scale, like the recent pandemic. When these big events happen, the world can feel scary and there may be lots of uncertainty. Suddenly, through no fault of your own, your life has to change and you feel like you have very little control over what is happening. Plans get cancelled, you have to miss school and you may not be able to do your normal activities for a while. It can actually feel like your world has been turned upside down!

You might also experience huge emotions during this time, depending on the situation. It might be fear, anxiety or sadness. Whatever you feel during times like these, just allow it to be there and remind yourself that these challenging thoughts and feelings are not permanent. This is a good time to ask for support and help from your loved ones. If you feel like you have no one to talk to, there are outside organisations that will help you, and they are listed in the back of this book. Just look for the helpers! Whenever the experience is big, remember to turn to the big people in your life:

the adults. You can also help yourself by doing the breathing practices that we have already talked about and look at all the tools that you have in your bag of tricks that will help you through.

 The situation may feel like it is out of your control, but you can focus on the things that you can control, like your breathing, or what you are eating, or making sure you are getting enough sleep. Self-care and kindness to yourself during these challenging times is the first priority. Just be gentle with yourself and look after yourself like you would your best friend. If you are worried about a loved one or even strangers across the world, you can still send them your positive love and intentions. The best way to do this is in a meditation practice, so read through the details below and give this a go.

 Start by closing your eyes and taking three deep breaths.

Breathe in through your nose and out through your mouth. Feel the rise and fall of your stomach or chest.

Give yourself permission to relax and choose to connect with your breath now.

Now, just work with your natural breath, there is no need to change your breath in any way.

Let your breath be the anchor.

I would like you to imagine that you are out in the middle of a beautiful green field. The grass is lush beneath your feet and above you is a perfect blue sky. The air is fresh and you can feel the warmth of the sun on the top of your head. Imagine this beautiful golden sunlight now coming in through the top of your head. This light is warm and filled with radiant health and love. Allow this light to fill your head. It fills up your eyes, ears, nose and mouth. Breathe in this golden light.

This beam of light now moves down through your neck and runs down into your shoulders, your arms and right to the tips of your fingers.

This light moves down into your chest now, filling your heart with a warm golden love. It runs down into your stomach and hips, through to your thighs, into your calf muscles and then finally into your feet, right to the tips of your toes.

This warm, golden light now fills every cell of your body. It fills your body with radiant health and wellbeing.

Allow yourself to just lie in the warmth of this light, allow it to soak into every cell within you.

And now, you can send this feeling of love and light out to your friends and family. Send this radiant health and wellbeing out to your community and to the world. And just lie here now and enjoy a feeling of calm.

Now gently come back to your breath again and the room that you are in. Start wiggling your fingers and toes and reconnect with your body and when you are ready just open your eyes.

Unexpected detours may take our adventures off course, but keep in mind that one day soon, we will be able to steer back around and carry on with our journey. Yes, things may have changed but hopefully we will be stronger and more resilient as a result.

BIG, GREY CLOUDS

When pilots are in the sky, they can't avoid all the big, grey clouds. They simply learn to fly their planes straight through them. We can think about our own personal challenges in the same way, like big, grey clouds in the sky. We don't really know when they will appear, but we can prepare ourselves so that when they do show up, we are strong enough to fly through them.

Please remember that clouds don't go on forever! Eventually, a plane does come out of the clouds and back into the **bright, sunny sky, and we will too.** Sometimes it just takes time and lots of support from our loved ones before we connect with the brightness of life again.

This is exactly what it felt like for me when I was working my way through depression. Every morning, it felt like I had a big, grey cloud directly above my head (actually, it was more like it surrounded my entire body!). But eventually, **I came through it** and now I love nothing more than to soak in the sunshine of life and help others do the same. When you come up against those big, grey clouds, **be kind to yourself** and have faith that the clouds will eventually move on.

You may have heard the saying:

And it's so true. You might not be able to find the silver lining straight away, but don't stop looking for it. When I think about my depression and all that I went through, I can now see that my silver lining was that it led me to do the work I do now. And I get to work with beautiful people like yourself every single day!

Overcoming challenges takes a lot of courage, so with that in mind I think it's time to tune into another episode of **UP AND AWAY.**

UP AND AWAY

with BETHANY HAMILTON

You may already know the story of Bethany Hamilton? It's an amazing story of both **courage** and **persistence.**

In 2003, Bethany was considered to be an up-and-coming surfer. One day, she was out surfing with her best friend, Alana, and Alana's dad Holt, when she was attacked by a tiger shark. She was 13 years old at the time and it changed her life forever. After being saved by Holt and rushed to hospital, **Bethany lost her left arm.**

For a short time after, she also felt like she had lost her dream of becoming a world champion surfer. She went through so many challenges during her recovery, including coming to terms with the fact that surfing would never be the same for her again. **But she did not give up.**

In fact, she was back out surfing within a month of the attack and won her first national surfing title less than two years later. Incredibly, by the time she was 17 years old, Bethany had reached her dream of becoming a professional surfer.

Bethany continues to inspire so many people around the world with her story of courage and belief.

But this is also a story of persistence.

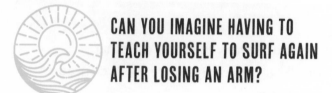 ## CAN YOU IMAGINE HAVING TO TEACH YOURSELF TO SURF AGAIN AFTER LOSING AN ARM?

Just think about balancing on a surfboard or paddling out in the water with one arm, and you can begin to understand how much determination this must have taken.

Bethany's dream of becoming a professional surfer faced many challenges along the way. However, she had a **vision for herself** and that kept her going despite the difficulties she experienced.

It really is an amazing story and I would highly recommend watching *Soul Surfer*, the movie of Bethany's experience, along with her new movie *Unstoppable,* which is incredibly inspiring!

> 'Courage doesn't mean you don't get afraid.
> Courage means you don't let the fear stop you.'
>
> — Bethany Hamilton

BOUNCE BACK

COURAGE

Can you think of a time when you had to find the courage to do something?

As Bethany says, 'Courage doesn't mean you don't get afraid. Courage means you don't let the fear stop you.'

Can you think of a time when you felt really scared of something but you managed to find the **courage to do it anyway**? It might have been making a presentation at school or even taking off on your first plane ride. Actually, it reminds me of the first time I went in a helicopter when I was 38 years old. **I am very scared of heights!** We were sitting in the helicopter, myself, my husband and the pilot. The pilot could obviously tell that I was a bit scared so he turned to me and asked, **'How are you feeling?'** to which I replied, **'A little bit scared, this is my first time in a helicopter.'** Guess what he said to me? **'Don't worry, it's mine too!'** How funny! It obviously wasn't the truth but by making that joke, the pilot helped me take my mind off being scared.

Can you think of a time when you were scared but you went ahead and did it anyway? I want you to think about how you felt once you had achieved whatever it was you went ahead and did.

I bet it felt great! In fact, I'm pretty sure that it would have put a **huge smile on your face** and your chest may have puffed out with pride. When we give ourselves a little push and get past our fear to achieve something, it really can help us build our confidence. We think to ourselves,

'YAY, I DID IT!'

And you know what's even better? We then start asking ourselves, **'What else can I do?'** because we start believing we can achieve anything that we set our minds to. This, my friend, is why it's important to get out of your comfort zone because that's the place where you will begin to understand that you can do more than you ever imagined.

It's time to head over to your travel diary and think about a time when you showed courage. It doesn't have to be a big thing; it could be something small like trying a new food. Reflect on how it felt to be brave. Did it change the way you think in any way?

LUGGAGE STRAPS

Have you ever seen those big, stretchy luggage straps that people use to put around their suitcase?

Did you know that those things have an enormous amount of give? You and your friend could stand at opposite ends of a room and stretch it right out across the room (but please don't try this one at home!), and you know what would happen if you both let go at the same time? The strap would quickly **bounce back** together to its original size. You can pull and pull and pull some more, and then let it go and it will still come back to its original size.

This is a great way to remember the next word that I want to talk about, which is resilience.

RESILENCE BASICALLY MEANS TO 'BOUNCE BACK'. IT HAS TO DO WITH OUR ABILITY TO BOUNCE BACK FROM CHALLENGES.

That's where our luggage strap comes in. Sometimes, you might feel like you are being pulled and pulled by certain situations or challenges. It might feel like you are being pulled mentally, physically and emotionally and that you just can't be stretched any further. But eventually the pull is released and you do your best to bounce back, or to come back to your 'normal' state.

The good news is that resilience is a skill that you can develop, so when challenges do happen in your life, you have the ability to bounce back and keep moving forward.

Everything you are learning in this book will help you build resilience, particularly tools like **meditation** and making sure you have a **good support network** around you.

Through of all of this, it's good to remember that challenges are not permanent, they will come and go. There's another great saying to help you think about this:

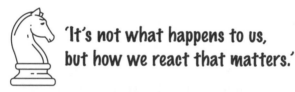 **'It's not what happens to us, but how we react that matters.'**

At the end of the day, we can't control the turbulence that we may face but we can choose how we respond to the turbulence.

This is such an important topic that I think it's worth diving into our next episode of **UP AND AWAY**, this time with Professor Andy McCann. Andy helps people build their resilience, so that when they face challenges or setbacks, they are able to bounce back.

UP AND AWAY

with ANDY McCANN

Q. Why is resilience important?

A. There are lots of different ways to explain what resilience is, but really it is an ability to adapt to change, difficulties and even distressing experiences. It is a key factor in protecting and promoting good mental health. The more someone shows resilience, the better they are at getting through tough times. We all experience tough times through life, so resilience is something that helps everyone.

Q. What are your top tools when it comes to building resilience?

A. The good news is that experts agree that skills that help us with our resilience can be learnt, and that general attitudes and behaviours are important. Resilience is not an end point, like passing an exam, but is something we are always working to try and have. It is the product of a number of mutually enhancing protective factors and I call these the basics of resilience.

BIOLOGY

Be aware of how you are feeling. When we experience difficult situations (with peers, in school, at home) our body releases a chemical cocktail that can make us feel uncomfortable. Finding out more about our biology, and why and what happens to our brain and body at such times, can be very reassuring.

ATTITUDE

Be aware of how you are thinking. In times of difficulty, thinking that everything is bad and everything always will be bad is called '**generalising thinking**' and should be challenged. Considering positive questions such as 'What did someone do today to make me feel happy?' and 'What did I do today to make someone else feel happy?' can be a useful activity to do.

SELF-CARE

Self-care is about:

Sleep

Exercise

Learning

Food

as they all have an amazingly positive effect on mental health and resilience. Learning about the effect of doing these small, positive things well, lots of times, is a key aspect of resilience.

RESILIENCE IS A TEAM SPORT!

'We need healthy relationships to be at our most resilient.'

— Andy McCann

INNER CONTROL

Resilience means understanding that you can't always have what you want as soon as you want it. This requires activities that help us recognise triggers that cause mood shifts and help us practise impulse control, turn-taking, patience and mental flexibility. We should take time to learn from mistakes.

CIRCUIT BREAKERS

We all naturally show more resilience in some situations than in others. Knowing how to 'break the mental circuit', so we don't take emotions from one situation to another, is useful. Breathing strategies and visualisation can help with these transitions.

SOCIAL SUPPORT

Resilience is a team sport! We need physical supplies (food and warmth) and social supplies (healthy relationships with friends, family and teachers) to be at our most resilient. We should put effort into relationships with others.

Q. Do you have any inspiring stories that you can share about bouncing back from challenges?

A. Maintaining or developing resilience is a personal journey. Winter Vinecki set and achieved her goal of running a marathon on every continent before she turned 15. She even set the record for the youngest person to do so. She did it in honour of her father, who had died of an aggressive form of cancer.

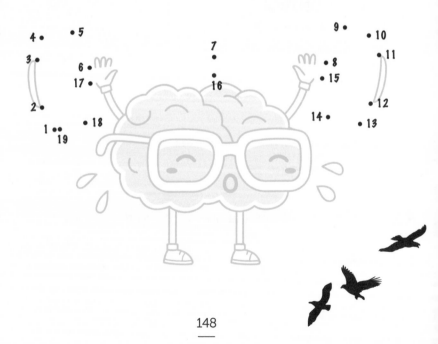

LITTLE THINGS

PONDER

It's time for us to ponder. Isn't that a great word? It's up there with 'wonder'. There is something so enticing about these two words. But what does ponder mean?

 TO PONDER IS TO REFLECT.

You have come a long way and I hope that you have been introduced to lots of new ideas and different ways of thinking about things.

Right now you may have **more questions than answers** and that's a good thing because it means that you are taking it all in and pondering.

Being on a plane and flying up high in the sky is the perfect opportunity to ponder. As you look out of the window, you reflect on the place and the people you have just left and think about **all the opportunities that await you** at your destination. Nothing is certain but you know that in this moment things have changed. **You are on your way to something new!** I would love you to stop and ponder what you have learnt so far and reflect on whether there have been any 'light bulb moments' for you? For example, you may have read something like 'your thoughts are not facts' and you thought:

 'Wow, I have never thought of it like that!'

Or you may have given more thought to excess baggage. Perhaps you have realised that there are certain bags that you are dragging around that it might be a good time to let go of?

 **Take some time now to ponder the main points that you have learnt so far.** Feel free to draw some pictures if you would prefer.

CHANGE IN DIRECTION

 I want you to give yourself a big pat on the back!

So far, we have talked about some pretty heavy topics, stuff like worry and stress, that most of us don't normally sit around and discuss.

It might not be your normal everyday conversation, but these things are super important.

 I HOPE THAT ONE DAY WE ARE ALL JUST AS COMFORTABLE DISCUSSING WHAT'S HAPPENING INSIDE OUR HEADS AS WE ARE DISCUSSING WHAT WE HAD FOR BREAKFAST.

We talk about our physical health (and diet!) on a regular basis, so why not our mental health as well?

For now, it's time to take a turn to the right and start talking about when things are going well (or should that be right?). Let's start with a quote:

 'Where your attention goes, your energy flows.'

That might sound a little confusing but what it means is what we focus on grows. So, if we are constantly putting our attention on all the things that go wrong or all the things that we don't have, then guess what? We are going to see more of that.

But, on a more positive note, if we start noticing what is going right, then it makes sense that this will grow instead.

Have you ever woken up in the morning, not felt great and thought to yourself, **'Uh-oh. It's going to be one of those days?'** and then, like some spell has been cast upon you, you drop your tablet, get in trouble and your teacher tells you that you aren't trying hard enough, all before recess!

It's literally like things go from bad to worse.

WOULDN'T IT BE NICE IF WE COULD TURN IT ALL AROUND?

Well, you absolutely can! You can start training yourself to change things around.

What's the secret?
Well, a really good place to start is with the practice of gratitude.

GRATITUDE

It is easy to feel grateful when you are going on a family holiday or it's your birthday or Christmas is just around the corner. The real trick to gratitude is trying to be thankful even when things aren't going as planned.

But let me back up a little bit. **Do you know what gratitude actually is?**

A big part of it is being able to say 'thank you', but there's a lot more to it than that.

 ## GRATITUDE IS ALSO A POSITIVE EMOTION.

If we are mindful enough, we can begin to notice this wonderful feeling in our body. Many people I have worked with have said that they feel gratitude in their heart area, and I know that's where I feel it the most too.

 See if you can sense where you feel gratitude in your body.

Read the instructions on the next page and then give this practice a go.

Close your eyes and take a nice big breath in through your nose and out through your mouth.

Take two more of these nice deep breaths and give yourself permission to relax.

Now I want you to think of someone who you are really grateful to have in your life. It could be Mum, Dad or your best friend.

Just think about that person and reflect on why you are so thankful for them.

Think about all the things that they have helped you do and all the times they have shown you love and kindness.

Just notice now where you feel this gratitude in your body. Is it in your chest area or is it somewhere else?

Simply notice, and you might like to send your love and blessings to the person you have been thinking about.

Then, when you are ready, open your eyes.

TRAVEL CALM

If you have ever experienced motion sickness, you will know it's not much fun. Actually, just the thought of it is enough to make me feel nauseous. If you do get sick travelling, you might be given something to counteract it, like Travelcalm, which usually does the trick. Even better, if you take the medicine before you start your travels, it prevents you from getting ill at all.

When we make **gratitude a daily habit,** it can be like a remedy to those more challenging emotions that we feel from time to time. It's a bit like Travelcalm: it can help you calm strong emotions.

When you are in a genuine state of gratitude, it's harder to notice fear or worry at the same time. Instead, you can choose to tune into **feelings of love and appreciation.**

Going back to our initial idea of **'what we focus on grows',** wouldn't it be lovely if we could keep growing these positive emotions instead?

GRATITUDE IS LITERALLY A GIFT THAT WE CAN <u>GIVE TO OURSELVES AND OTHERS.</u>

With this in mind, I want you to take a minute now and think about some of the things that you are grateful for in your own life.

GRATITUDE ALPHABET

In your diary, write the alphabet down one side of the page. Then next to each letter, I want you list something that you are grateful for that begins with that letter. For example:

A: Air, B: Bed

MAGICAL MEMORIES

Ahhh, holidays. For the most part, they really do bring out the best in people. If you are lucky enough to have experienced a family holiday, this is something to be grateful for in itself. Remember, not everyone can go on holidays, so it really isn't something that we should take for granted. If you are one of the lucky ones who has experienced a family holiday, doesn't it seem like everyone makes a super effort to have a nice time? Siblings try not to argue (yes, I know that can be hard!) and parents try not to get upset if things go wrong.

Why is that? Simple, really. Holidays are usually considered 'precious' time together and who wants to ruin 'precious' time with arguments and by focusing on what's going wrong? That doesn't mean that it won't happen of course, but I do think people make more of an effort to be **happy and have fun** when they are on holidays.

It makes sense when you think about how hard people work. When the opportunity for a break comes around, of course people want to try to make the most of it. You may have also noticed that adults take more photos when they're on holiday? It's like they want to keep a record of this special family time.

I like to call them magical memories.

THEY ARE THE MEMORIES THAT YOU WANT TO KEEP FOREVER.

In our family, we take these 'magical memories' one step further. We have a jar in our living room and every time something good happens to any of us, we write it on a piece of paper and pop it into the jar. It could be something that we have achieved individually, or it could be a nice moment that we have shared as a family. Yes, it could be a memory from a family holiday, but we also like to use this jar to record the little, everyday things such as a **good belly laugh** or a family bike ride on a **sunny morning.**

And guess what?

When you know you are collecting these magical memories, you find yourself looking for them.

A picnic at the park suddenly becomes much more than a picnic in the park—it becomes something that you pay attention to and don't take for granted. And you know what the best bit of this whole thing is?

You can start right now!

Don't wait for something 'big' to happen, start with the small things and you will soon notice how much there is for you to be grateful for.

Can you remember all the way back to the first part of this book when we were talking about the negativity bias? That is, that the human mind is hardwired to look for what is going wrong? Well, this is why simple things, such as having a Magical Memories jar, can make a big difference.

IT HELPS US TO TRAIN OUR MINDS TO FOCUS ON WHAT'S GOING WELL INSTEAD OF WHAT'S GOING WRONG.

What types of things would go into your Magical Memories jar?

Magical Memories

You can also create 'future magical memories' for yourself. At times when things seem challenging or you feel like you are missing someone or something, write a 'future' magical memory of seeing that person or doing that activity and add it to the jar. This gives you the opportunity to acknowledge what is important and invite it into your life!

To take this idea one step further, you can always close your eyes and on the movie screen in your mind, picture that person or activity that you would like to do.

Use your imagination to add as much detail and colour to this movie and make it come alive.

Remember, you have the power to create your own headventure and just notice how it makes you feel on the inside.

IN THE ZONE

SMOOTH FLYING

Have you ever felt like things were just cruising along? Maybe things were going super well, without too much stress or worry? This is really what I want you to experience, or at least recognise, in your own life. It's most likely that you've had moments where things felt really great. **When you have felt content and happy.** But it's also likely that these moments slipped past you quickly, without you giving them any real attention. **Why is that?** Remember, our brains are hardwired to look for what is going wrong.

This is why it's incredibly important to try to savour the good times. Next time you notice something good happening (remember to include the small things), try this:

Recognise when something good is happening and stay with the experience for 30 seconds.

Focus all your attention on what is happening around you and within you.

Notice everything you can about the experience—the colours, the taste, smells and sounds and try to soak in the good feeling.

Imagine the good feeling sinking deep into your body.

Then notice how you feel on the inside. It might help to close your eyes so that you are not distracted.

Just pay attention to how your body feels and also your mind. Give yourself permission to soak in the good feelings.

Not only does this little exercise help us feel good, but when you can savour an experience for about 30 seconds, you are also creating new neural pathways in your brain—**you are literally starting to rewire your brain for happiness!**

IN FLOW

There are also times when you may feel completely 'in flow'. You might have heard athletes or performers use the term in flow or 'in the zone'. Basically, this is a state that we can go into when we are doing an activity we love.

I think of flow as a **'meditation in motion'** because it can almost feel like you are meditating while you are moving about. It could be a certain sport—surfing or cycling are great examples. Or you might go into flow when you are writing, painting or even cooking.

Think about your own life. Has there ever been a time when you were so involved in an activity, you literally lost track of time? For me, it is either writing or being active in nature. Time seems to disappear and I feel so connected to the moment.

CHANCES ARE THAT YOU ENTERED A FLOW STATE.

Have a look at the indicators below. This will help you decide if you have been in a flow state because when you are, you usually experience the following:

You lose track of time • You are active
you are not overthinking or thinking about yourself
you are quietly confident • you work effortlessly
you are in a state of bliss

Once you recognise what you were doing when you felt in the flow state, the trick is to do it more often. **Ultimately, this is when we humans are happiest.** Find what activity it is for you and do more of it! When we are in flow, we feel good. When we feel good, we do good. When we do good, we get good results and contribute to the world in a positive way. This really is the next level way of doing things!

WHAT LIGHTS YOU UP?

FIRST-CLASS ATTITUDE

Forget business class! When it comes to **choosing** your attitude, go first class every time. I emphasise **choosing** here because it really is a choice, although many of us don't realise it.

As we've already discovered, we might not be able to control everything that happens to us but we can choose how we react to it. By choosing to have a first-class attitude, we make sure we are responding in a way that serves **us** the best.

Have you ever been told that you have a bad attitude or that your attitude needs to change? Don't worry, there are plenty of us who have! This is usually a pretty good sign that you might need to change something. Every time you hear something along these lines, it might help to picture this . . .

Ask yourself this question 'What is the next RIGHT action I can take?'

Strong emotions, such as anger, fear, disappointment and frustration, can often contribute to a 'bad attitude' but rather than use these as a way to justify your attitude, try to use them as a signal to take action.

For example, you might be at school and someone makes a mean comment about your performance in a lesson. The comments really hurt you and have embarrassed you in front of your classmates. When you finally walk away from the situation, you realise that you are now feeling very angry and your mind turns to how you could get that person back. But consider the bigger picture (like the general rules of society!), do you think deliberately setting out to hurt the other person in order to get revenge is the next RIGHT action? The short answer is NO, even if that's how the anger is making you feel in the moment. Often, we can put all our energy and focus back onto the person who has hurt us when we should be using our energy to make **ourselves** feel better.

SO, THE NEXT RIGHT ACTION SHOULD BE ABOUT CARING FOR YOURSELF.

If you feel hurt, it's OK to cry and let it out. If you feel angry, it's OK to go and do some star jumps to release some of that energy, or have a shower or bath to refresh and reset. Just recognise that those feelings are there for a reason. If you are feeling angry, it could be your body's way of letting you know that someone has just crossed a boundary. Take some time to acknowledge how you are feeling and sit with it. You could even do some breathing to help those feelings to subside.

Having a first-class attitude really comes down to making choices that help you.

 Could you go and do an activity that you love to help you feel better?

Could you take five minutes to go outside and sit under a tree? Activities like these will help bring you back to neutral, rather than staying in a cycle of anger and hostility.

#1 RULE FOR LIFE: Take good care of you!

AMENITY KITS

While we are on the topic of first class, have you ever seen one of the amenity kits that you get when you are a first-class passenger? They are filled with amazing lotions and potions, with the main aim being that you will feel at your best when the plane lands. I can't say I have had the pleasure of flying first class but that doesn't mean that I can't look after myself!

 **SELF-CARE IS ESSENTIAL. PUT ON YOUR OWN OXYGEN MASK FIRST.**

Self-care is so important. From the little things like brushing your teeth regularly to the bigger things like getting enough sleep and drinking enough water, you can't overestimate the importance of taking good care of yourself.

At your age, sleep is one of the most important things that you can be doing for the development of your body and brain. I know it may not feel like you are doing much when you are pumping out those **Zs** at night, but without it, life can be a struggle. Have you ever had a late night and then found it hard to focus and concentrate in class the next day?

It's a good idea to come up with your own self-care plan. To help you do this, I have included a few ideas below. You'll notice that this is divided up into mind, body, spirit and heart, as this can make it a lot easier to think about. It's important that we take good care of all aspects of ourselves, not just our body.

Self-care plan

MIND

be creative
take breaks
read
problem solve
learn new things

BODY

drink water
eat healthily
relax
do deep breathing
exercise

SPIRIT

be in nature
meditate
help others
sing, dance
practise mindfulness

HEART

have fun
laugh
cuddle a pet
visit friends
see family

Once you have had a look at the ideas in the picture above, it's your turn to come up with your own self-care plan.

 Draw the table illustrated below into your diary and have a think about what types of things you would include in each area.

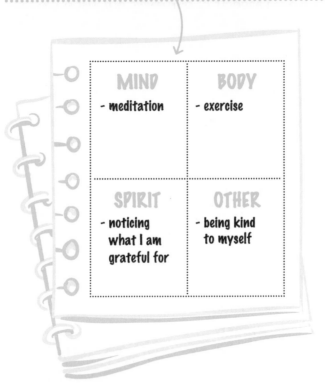

MIND	BODY
- meditation	- exercise

SPIRIT	OTHER
- noticing what I am grateful for	- being kind to myself

Great work! It's really up to you now to make this part of your own first-class journey. Try to do these things on a regular basis so that you feel at your best.

 Choose one thing that you will do today.

This is your one and only reminder that you are a ...

VERY. IMPORTANT. PERSON

and that your life is a ...

VERY. IMPORTANT. PROJECT

You really do owe it to yourself to treat yourself like a V.I.P. I don't mean that you have to have all the latest stuff in order to feel good. Sure, a smartphone can be handy but it really won't make you a better or 'cooler' person. Nor will the new trainers, the latest branded T-shirt or living in the biggest house. Forget the 'stuff' for now and focus on what's really important: feeling good on the inside. **Self-care is a great place to start!** Start treating yourself like a V.I.P because you deserve it. Don't wait for other people to do it for you, otherwise it may never happen. Start recognising what makes you feel good and start doing it.

Here's the thing: when we feel good, it's a lot easier for us to 'do good', for ourselves and others. Let's take a look at two different scenarios and you can judge for yourself.

1
You choose to go to bed late, argue with parents and then don't sleep very well.

2
It's time to get up and you are feeling tired (and cranky!). You choose to ignore Mum when she asks you to get dressed.

SCENARIO 1.

4
You finally head to school knowing you have upset Mum and Dad. (And you forget to brush your teeth!)

3
You're really not feeling great so when Dad asks you to give him a hand to take the rubbish out you quickly snap 'no'.

Can you relate to Scenario 1? No? What about Scenario 2 then?

1
You choose to go to bed on time and get a great night's sleep.

2
It's time to get up and you are feeling so energised that you quickly get dressed and decide to do some push-ups in the backyard.

SCENARIO 2.

4
You head to school in a great mood, knowing that you've made a positive difference this morning. (And you also remembered to brush your teeth!)

3
Dad asks you to give him a hand with the rubbish and you literally bounce into action.

Which scenario do you think makes you feel better? Maybe it's not even a case of 'better', it's just that the second scenario could certainly help make a person feel good, as opposed to the first scenario.

Can you see once again that it all comes down to a matter of choice?

 What choices are you making?

YOUR HEART SONG

NOISE-CANCELLING HEADPHONES

I'm sure you already know this, but our daily lives can be filled with a great deal of noise. You'll no doubt have parents telling you how to do things, teachers giving you lots more information, and then friends and frenemies also sharing their opinions. Yes, some of this noise is useful and can help you to learn new ways of doing things but some of it may be unwanted or harmful.

On this journey to taking your life to the next level, it pays to have some noise-cancelling headphones. These can simply be an imaginary piece of equipment that you choose to put on when you notice other people trying to put you down.

If there is one thing I have come to realise over the years, it is that:

 **HUMANS ARE VERY QUICK TO JUDGE EACH OTHER.**

In fact, research shows that it only takes about seven seconds for us to judge another person, and that's without them even saying a word! We constantly judge others and of course we also get judged too. Have you ever felt somebody just look you up and down? It's not very pleasant. We judge each other on the way we look, what we wear, what we say, how we act, where we live, what team we barrack for, and the list goes on.

I would love to be able to say to young people (and even adults) 'please don't judge' but it's just not that easy. What we can do is become aware that this is happening and simply notice when we have gone into 'judgement mode'. When you notice someone judging you unfairly, it's a good time to slip on those imaginary noise-cancelling headphones and move on.

Just remember that when people are judging you, it really says more about them as a person than you: something within them is uncomfortable. Wouldn't it be nice if we could just accept each other instead?

Next time you find yourself in judgement mode, you could try saying this instead:

 **I give myself 100% permission to be myself right now and I give others 100% permission to be themselves.**

And simply let the judgements go. We can actually waste a lot of our time and energy judging or just even thinking about other people. This is time and energy that we could be using on ourselves instead. Let's make it our mission to just accept others they are; simple as that.

INNER COMPASS

We all have what I call our **inner compass.** When the noise overwhelms you, another option is to tune in to your inner compass and let it guide you in the direction you need to go.

YOUR INNER COMPASS KNOWS WHAT IS BEST—YOU JUST HAVE TO TRAIN YOURSELF TO TAKE NOTICE OF IT.

You may already know the words 'intuition' or 'gut feeling'. These are other ways of describing our inner compass. Have you ever had a sense that you were going to run into someone you know down the street or that something was about to happen? Well, guess what? That was your inner compass.

The first step to tuning in to your inner compass is learning to calm your mind. It sounds easy, but this is where many of us struggle. Remember, our minds are extremely busy so this is where meditation really comes in handy.

Meditation will help slow things down and eventually you will be able to hear the voice of your heart instead.

Your heart is home to your inner compass, and this is a voice that will usually whisper rather than shout. We all have that voice within us and we just need to remind ourselves how to tune in.

Let's do a little practice to help you to connect with it. The trick with this is not to overthink it. Your intuition is usually the first answer that springs into your awareness, not the one that you want to come up with after five minutes of tossing other options out!

 Sit on the floor or in a chair and just close your eyes.

Take in a nice big breath through your nose and out through the mouth.

Then take two more nice deep breaths in through the nose and out through the mouth.

Give yourself permission to relax and take your time.

When you feel yourself relax or your body feels looser, ask yourself three questions quietly in your mind:

1 *My mind needs . . .?*

2 *My body needs . . .?*

3 *My spirit needs . . .?*

Notice what answers you come up with. I like to think of my 'spirit' as simply the energy of my next level self.

It's that part of you that holds all your hopes and dreams for the future.

When you are ready, return to your breath and gently open your eyes.

You might like to write down what answers you came up with.

As I mentioned, the first answer that pops into your awareness is usually the right one. Don't forget that things change, so if you repeat this practice in a week's time, your answers might be completely different.

Your inner compass is there to help guide you in the present moment. It can help you with small things or bigger decisions but remember to get yourself into a relaxed or neutral state first. An essential part of being able to tune in to your inner compass is being able to quieten the noise of your mind.

LISTEN TO YOUR HEART:
it will guide you.

I WONDER...

I want to invite you to try a practice that uses your inner compass to answer some fun **'I wonder'** questions. Do you remember the word 'wonder' from earlier? It's about approaching things with a sense of joy, excitement and curiosity. So instead of saying something like, 'I must . . .' we can say, 'I wonder . . .' instead. Can you see by changing the statement, it becomes less serious and makes you curious as opposed to anxious?

Take some deep breaths and get yourself into a nice neutral state.

Give yourself permission to relax and enjoy this practice.

Read through the questions and, with your eyes closed, see what answers or images you receive:

1. *I wonder what my life will be like one year from now?*

2. *I wonder what I'll look like in five years from now?*

3. *I wonder how I can make a positive contribution to the world*

4. *I wonder what amazing experiences I will have in my future?*

I wonder what happened for you during that practice. I hope you received some insight. If you didn't, don't be concerned. Remember that sometimes all it takes is a little bit of practice. Just try and have a bit of fun with it and relax. The more relaxed you are, the easier it will be.

NEW EXPERIENCES

Travel is all about having new experiences. It is an opportunity to meet new people, taste new foods and embrace new and different ways of living.

What many of us don't realise is that you don't have to travel to the other side of the world to achieve this. Sometimes, all it takes is going to a different park or beach to have a new and wonderful experience.

I want you to think of every day as an opportunity to have a new adventure. A word of warning here though: it will require you to put your device down, open the front door and actually take a step outside! Can you do that? I say this jokingly but at the same time I am being 100% serious. I hear (and see) far too many bright, fun-loving young people spend all their time on a device when there is literally a world of adventure out there. **So please, go and take a look!**

When we look for adventure, it opens the door to creativity, inspiration and it's also good for your mind, body and spirit. Opening yourself up to new experiences will work wonders when it comes to combating the good old b-word, which is, of course, **boredom.**

I want you to have a think about how you could have some new experiences, starting today. Here are a few ideas to help get your creative juices flowing:

try a new food learn a language
change your hairstyle **learn a new skill**
sit with a different group during lunch
make a cubbyhouse **go on a bushwalk**
try a new exercise **cook dinner for your family**
do a random act of kindness
borrow someone's pet for a day

We are here to have these new experiences—they keep us feeling connected and alive. They help us understand what we love to do and what makes us feel good inside. Seeking out new experiences can also teach us a lot about ourselves. What types of things are you attracted to? What types of experiences do you keep away from and why? Sometimes we get stuck in the same old routine, doing the same old thing, and that's when life can feel pretty boring and uninteresting. However, it's the times when we feel a bit restless that we should deliberately try and find something new to experience.

The isolation during the pandemic has really high-lighted this for many children and adults. Some saw it as an opportunity to try out new things at home, while others felt bored without being able to go out, or keep up their normal, busy routines. I believe that:

 ## BOREDOM IS REALLY A CALL TO ACTION.

It's your spirit letting you know that you feel unfulfilled and wanting you to seek out something new. Rather than feel sorry for yourself, sit with the boredom and be curious around what ideas might pop into your head. Unleash your imagination—don't fill every minute with a device! How are you ever going to think of something new if your mind is being distracted by TV or iPads? I encourage you to put the devices down and just sit with your boredom and ask yourself:

 ## 'What can I create in this space?'

It seems like such a simple question but many of us don't ask it. Give yourself a chance to get bored so that you can see what else is possible for you.

 ## WHAT ELSE IS OUT THERE THAT WOULD MAKE YOUR HEART SING WITH JOY?

PUTTING YOURSELF OUT THERE

I don't know about you, but all of this raises a question for me: **Why do we find it so hard to try new things?** Part of it is due to fear, as we have discussed earlier, and that we don't really want to step outside our comfort zone. Our comfort zone keeps us feeling safe, but it also means we aren't really stretching ourselves. In order to grow mentally, emotionally and physically, we have to be able to step outside of that comfort. This means accepting that feeling uncomfortable is totally OK. In fact, it means you are growing as a person!

 Putting yourself out there is about embracing the courage that I know you have inside of you.

It's about giving yourself a little nudge and saying, 'You've got this!' and then giving it your best shot. It comes down to taking action, which we need to do in order to achieve anything.

To help you out a little more with this, I got in touch with the 'Queen of Action', Mel Robbins. For those of you who don't know, Mel has her own TV show in the US and is well known for her book called *The 5 Second Rule*. This is a brilliant little 'hack' for getting yourself up and going when you are feeling fear or just stuck. So, it's time for another episode of **UP AND AWAY!**

UP AND AWAY

with MEL ROBBINS

Q. **How can young people use the 5 second rule to help them get going?**

A. First, the 5 Second Rule is a tool that helps you interrupt the thoughts that tell you something is too hard, or you don't feel like it, or you're afraid. But it's also a starting ritual, so when you count back 5-4-3-2-1 and then MOVE, your brain gets programmed to take action every time you count back from five. Keep using the rule, and you build new and better habits.

Q. **Why is it important to 'put ourselves out there'?**

A. You have to live at least part of your life in what I call 'the uncomfort zone', because that is where all the good stuff happens. This is where you try new things, learn more about yourself and learn about life in general. The more you step into this zone, the more your confidence builds.

Q. **What are your thoughts on dealing with fear?**

A. We can be afraid and still do the things that scare us, and there's a trick I use that helps you turn fear into excitement. To a brain, fear and excitement feel the same in the body. So, the next time you start to feel afraid and your heart beats faster or your palms get sweaty, switch gears in your brain. Tell yourself that you're excited! You can't wait to do what you're about to do! Your brain will believe you and you'll have an easier time taking action.

Q. **What advice would you have loved to have heard as a 10- or 12-year-old?**

A. I wish someone had told me that it was OK to be me, exactly as I was. I thought the way to get other kids to like me was to be just like them and because I was always scared to be me, sometimes I was mean. But the way you get others to like you—the ones who matter—is to be the best YOU. Read what you want to read, like what you want to like, listen to what you want to listen to and most of all, always be kind.

Q. **Anything else you would like to share with our young readers?**

A. There are some days that it's hard being a kid but always remember that no matter how hard it gets, you always have the power to choose what you think and what you do.

'The uncomfort zone is where all the good stuff happens.'

— Mel Robbins

EVERYTHING IS PROGRESS

Mel makes such an important point:

Some days it's hard being a kid. But always remember that no matter how hard it gets, you always have the power to choose what you think and what you do.

You probably already understand that a journey is made up of countless steps. Some of those steps will be forward, in the direction of your dream, others might be more like a side-step or even a step backwards. **It doesn't matter!** Just remember that it's all progress, even the backwards ones. If you make a 'bad' choice, don't be too hard on yourself, just look for the lesson and keep moving forward and

 **KNOW THAT THE JOURNEY ISN'T MEANT TO BE PERFECT.**

It's actually perfectly imperfect! Most of the people who you admire for being successful didn't wake up one day being a huge success. They had to commit to their dream, work at it and stay focused.

Mel Robbins is a great example. She came up with the 5 Second Rule because she so desperately wanted to make changes in her own life. She literally used her

5-4-3-2-1 rule to get herself out of bed one morning and is now helping thousands of people do the same. I really admire her for that.

It doesn't matter where you are at the moment, just take the next step.

Use Mel's 5 Second Rule to help you get started, particularly if there is something that you are scared of doing or don't feel like doing. I can't emphasise this enough: if there is something you want to work towards then you **have** to commit to it. Yes, that means hanging in there when there is turbulence and there are setbacks. Just keep taking action because everything is progress!

THE JOURNEY OF A THOUSAND MILES
BEGINS WITH A SINGLE STEP.

PART THREE:

PREPARING FOR LANDING

KNOW YOURSELF

LADIES AND GENTLEMEN, AS WE START OUR DESCENT, PLEASE MAKE SURE YOUR SEAT BACKS AND TRAY TABLES ARE IN THEIR FULL UPRIGHT POSITION. MAKE SURE YOUR SEAT BELT IS SECURELY FASTENED AND ALL LUGGAGE IS STOWED UNDERNEATH THE SEAT IN FRONT OF YOU OR IN THE OVERHEAD BINS. THANK YOU.

Well, here we are. Landing in a new destination is both **exciting and nerve-wracking** at the same time. You may feel excited about all the possibilities and are filled with anticipation but at the same time, you might notice a few fears coming to the surface. Hopefully by now you know this is all part of the process and you can simply say to yourself, **'I've got this.'**

The plane ride might be coming to an end but your journey is only really just beginning. When the seatbelt sign goes off, it is time for you to unfasten the buckle— and it will be time for you to start taking your life to the next level.

But before you leave, there are a few more travel tips I want to share. These are things that will help you even more when your feet hit the ground and you are ready to go. This last part of your travel guide is really all about what to expect when you arrive and how to make the most of your journey from here.

Smile!
You are in the right place.

LOST IN TRANSLATION

I'll never forget my first experience of arriving in Rome in my early 20s with my sister. The plane landed and we were filled with excitement (and a few nerves). We collected our bags and off we went to catch a bus to the place that we were staying.

That's when it hit me: **'We actually can't communicate with anyone!'** In my ignorance, I hadn't even thought about the fact that everyone would be speaking in Italian. We tried to figure out the bus timetable, with no luck. We tried to ask people walking by: no luck. My excitement soon turned to fear as I realised that when you can't communicate properly, simple things can become extremely complicated. After a long delay, we finally found someone who could speak a little English and who was happy to help us catch the correct bus.

The moral of this story?

COMMUNICATION IS THE KEY TO BUILDING STRONG AND HEALTHY RELATIONSHIPS.

Have you ever thought about *how* you actually communicate with the people in your life? But before you jump in and do that, you may be wondering why on earth we are talking about other people, when this is meant to be *your* journey? Well, just like I had to rely on a complete stranger in Rome to help me get to my destination, you will also have to rely on many other people as you make the journey to becoming your, next level, self.

Parents, teachers, coaches, friends and, yes, even frenemies will all have an influence on your journey.

If we lack communication skills, it can have a negative impact on the quality of our relationships with the important people in our lives.

To help you better understand how you prefer to communicate, I want to introduce you to the concept of introverts and extroverts. Some of you may already know the difference but for those of you who don't, here is a quick summary:

Extrovert: extroverts love being with other people. They love to talk, make friends and basically are the 'life of the party'! Extroverts feel energised when they are with other people. They are usually quite loud and outgoing.

Introverts: introverts love being on their own. They enjoy their own company and find that time on their own is what gives them energy. Introverts can find being in large groups exhausting. While extroverts love to communicate face to face, introverts will often make great listeners and are more likely to think things through in their mind before speaking out loud.

After reading through the two summaries, do you have any idea what your communication style might be? **Are you more extroverted or introverted?** I also want to be clear here that there is no 'better' style. Just because introverts prefer to be on their own doesn't mean that there is something wrong with them! Some of the most creative and intelligent people in the world are introverts. Can you think of any?

There is also another style known as an **'ambivert',** which sits smack back in the middle. If you are an ambivert then good for you: you have the best of both worlds.

As I have already mentioned, there is no 'right' or 'wrong' when it comes to communication styles. This is more about getting to know your own style, as it can help shed some light on why you are the way you are when it comes to socialising and being around other people. I'll let you in on another little secret here: I am an introvert but I didn't actually realise this until I was in my 30s! I also have an older sister who is an extrovert.

When I was your age, I used to look at my sister and wonder what on earth was wrong with me. My inner critic would tell me, **'Why can't you be more popular?'** or **'Why are you so quiet, what's wrong with you?'** I wish someone had explained to me that I just had a different way of communicating with people. It could have saved me the grief that I put myself through, trying to be someone that I wasn't. Being an introvert doesn't mean that you are necessarily 'shy' either. It just means that you value your own company and that's what gives you energy. It's a good thing to realise that other people can drain your energy, but that doesn't mean you can use it as an excuse and avoid **all social situations** either! You just need to plan your time in advance and make sure you have some 'down time' before or after a social gathering.

IT'S STILL IMPORTANT TO GIVE YOURSELF A LITTLE NUDGE AND PUT YOURSELF OUT THERE IN THE BIG WIDE WORLD BECAUSE REMEMBER THAT IS HOW WE GROW.

Now for those of you who are extroverts, it's equally important for you guys to also have 'down time' and get used to **your own company.** Because extroverts get their energy from other people, they often struggle when they are on their own. So perhaps you guys can give yourself a little nudge and do this on a daily basis (is that a meditation bell I hear?). If you really have no idea which you lean towards, then you can go online and do a very short survey to find out: quietrev.com/the-introvert-test. This is a quiz that was developed by author and speaker Susan Cain, and while her quiz is not scientific, it is a very good measure of temperament.

If you are an introvert and would like to do some more reading around this topic then I can highly recommend a book by Susan called **Quiet Power: The Secret Strengths of Introverted Kids,** which is a teens guide to being an introvert. And just remember, regardless of what your style is . . .

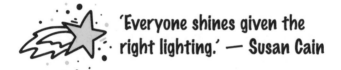

'Everyone shines given the right lighting.' — Susan Cain

Knowing your communication style will also help you to understand your preferences in how you actually communicate with the people in your life. If you are an introvert, you may prefer to write things in an email or a text message. You are less likely to want to communicate in a big group setting. However, if you are an extrovert, big groups are no problems at all. Actually, this is when you are at your best as you prefer to communicate with someone through face-to-face contact. This is handy information to keep in mind when you are meeting new people or you are trying to work through a conflict. First of all, recognise how you prefer to communicate and go from there.

MAKING A CHANGE

At this point in the journey, you might feel like there are one, two or many changes that you would like to make and are perhaps starting to think of ways to do this.

 **WHEN IT COMES TO CHANGE, IT'S GOOD TO REMEMBER THAT YOU MAY NOT SEE THE RESULTS STRAIGHT AWAY.**

For example, when a pilot needs to turn a jumbo jet left, they slowly veer the plane in a left direction but that plane doesn't turn left straight away. In fact, the turn is so slow and subtle that the passengers onboard often don't even realise that they have even changed direction. This is exactly how change works for us.

 **It can take time, so please be patient with yourself.**

Let me give you another example. Just say that you are an introvert and you have made a decision to put yourself out there a little bit more when it comes to socialising. There is a group activity that you have been invited to and rather than say, 'No, I am busy' like you normally would, you actually challenge yourself to go. The morning of the activity arrives and you feel yourself getting nervous about going but you know that it's important to stretch yourself, so you go. It doesn't feel easy for you—in fact, when you get home you say to your mum, 'It wasn't great' but you also are proud of yourself for doing it. Then the next time you get invited to go somewhere, it feels easier ... and before you know it, you have plans most weekends, and recognise how much you enjoy it. Just think, if you hadn't stuck with it, you would probably still be sitting at home wondering what everyone else is up to!

It might help to think of change as a process— something that happens over a period of time. If you are serious about making positive changes in your life, then, once again, you will need to stay focused and committed, as it can be very easy to be pulled off track!

Being an introvert myself, I know how easy it is to be drawn to my inner world of thoughts or spend time on my own reading or being in nature. What I have learnt over the years is that it's really all about balance. We need a little bit of everything to help us feel content!

Are you noticing what types of things you would like to change in your life? Take a few moments now to jot them down in your diary.

ARE WE THERE YET!

Can you remember when you were small asking your parents, **'Are we there yet?'** You might still ask it now, which is totally OK with me because what I'm really interested in here is the power of **'yet'**! Did you know that adding this simple word to the end of your sentence can help change the way you think about something? Let's investigate:

1) 'I can't play soccer' **versus**
'I can't play soccer yet.'

2) 'I'm not good at spelling' **versus**
'I'm not good at spelling yet.'

3) 'I don't understand maths' **versus**
'I don't understand maths yet.'

4) 'This doesn't work for me' **versus**
'This doesn't work for me yet.'

Can you see the difference? By simply adding a 'yet' to the end of these statements, you take the situation from being a challenge to becoming a possibility instead.

TRY THIS SIMPLE TOOL NEXT TIME YOU NOTICE YOUR INNER CRITIC TELLING YOU THAT SOMETHING CAN'T BE DONE . . . YET!

Quite often, we shut the door to new possibilities because we get stuck in a 'can't' mindset. I want you to understand that there is no harm in trying and just seeing what happens. You might try and fail (like we have talked about earlier) but don't be ashamed about failing.

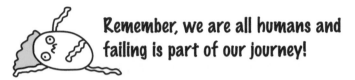 **Remember, we are all humans and failing is part of our journey!**

Allow yourself to remain open. Remember when you were younger and you were willing to try anything because you were just so curious? You weren't afraid of learning to walk, you weren't afraid of jumping in puddles—you just wanted the experience. Next time you have a chance to try something new, do it through the eyes of your younger self. This means not worrying about who is watching but really embracing a new opportunity. Allow yourself to enjoy it!

The power of YET!

SELFIES

For those of you that already use smartphones, I have no doubt that when you land, you will want to take a few selfies. It's a good way of recording your journey, right?

But you know what? I would love to introduce you to the only selfies that you should really ever worry about, and you don't need a smart device for any of these.

self-love   self-respect
self-determination   self-approval
self-belief   self-awareness   self-control
self-esteem   self-care   self-mastery

I'm guessing that this isn't **your idea of exciting social media content** but here's the thing:

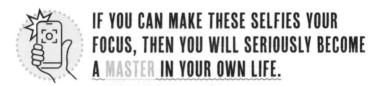 IF YOU CAN MAKE THESE SELFIES YOUR FOCUS, THEN YOU WILL SERIOUSLY BECOME A MASTER IN YOUR OWN LIFE.

These selfies are actually so important, I'd love for you to spend some time now thinking about what they actually mean to you.

Can you draw the following table into your diary and then have a think about what these words actually mean to you? You can even give them a score out of ten.

For example, if self-love is really important, you would score it 10/10 and if self-approval isn't as important, you might give it 6/10. If you need a bit of help understanding what some of these terms mean, it's a great opportunity to have a chat to your parents or an older adult if you can.

Self-love	/10
Self-respect	/10
Self-determination	/10
Self-approval	/10
Self-belief	/10
Self-awareness	/10
Self-control	/10
Self-esteem	/10
Self-care	/10
Self-mastery	/10

These words are all explained in the glossary at the back of the book.

When I am teaching Greatfulness, in the very first lesson I get everyone to take part in a 'values' exercise. During this activity, all the students stand in a circle and I call out different values, things like **'family', 'courage', 'independence'** and if a student 'values' what I have called out, they simply take a step into the circle. It never ceases to amaze me how few people step into the circle when I call out 'self-love'. It actually breaks my heart to see maybe five people out of a group of 70 students take a step in. I do remember what it was like when I was at school and you would be teased for 'loving yourself' but wouldn't it be nice if we could change that?

WOULDN'T IT BE NICE IF <u>LOVING YOURSELF</u> WAS THE COOL THING TO DO?

When I am talking about self-love, I don't mean just caring about your appearance and wearing the latest brand clothes. I am talking more about:

having regard for your own wellbeing and happiness.

Basically, making yourself a priority. Making it your job to take good care of you and really paying attention to what you need. Ultimately, this is what this whole book is about: helping you learn to love yourself exactly as you are, and becoming the best possible version of yourself, to realise that this is possible AND that you deserve it, regardless of where you are in your life at the moment. **There is so much potential inside of you, right now.**

NEXT LEVEL SELF

Just close your eyes for a minute and imagine your best self. This could be the future you or it could be you right now. Spend some time getting to know the next level you. Remember, this isn't about creating a 'perfect' you—there is no such thing as perfect. This is about embracing every aspect of yourself and shining a light on your strengths. What are you like when you are at your best? Do you know? Have a think about the questions below and just allow yourself to imagine how the best version of you thinks, feels and behaves.

1. How do you think?

2. How do you feel?

3. How do you behave?

4. How do you present yourself to the world?

Draw an image of the next level you in your diary. Or you can cut pictures out of magazines or print images you find online to create an idea of how you would like to think, feel, and be.

Create a vision of yourself, for yourself.

Being beautiful means being yourself so make it your mission to find out what that means to you. It's totally OK to be different.

BE-YOU-TIFUL!

WHY FIT IN?

WE ALL HAVE WINGS

There are so many different kinds of plane in the world that it seems impossible to keep count of them all. Most of us just accept that there are lots of different planes and that there are probably very good reasons why there are so many.

Each plane offers something different. There are all sorts of passenger planes, cargo planes and many variations of the military plane. Every plane serves a purpose. We humans are no different.

As you already know, I believe that each of us has a unique reason for being here, that there is something that each of us will offer and contribute to the world over the course of our lives. A big part of discovering what this is starts with accepting that we are all different. More importantly, that being different is a good thing—it's actually your superpower!

Imagine if we were all copies of each other. The world would be a boring (not to mention weird) place. The fact that we all have something different to offer is the reason that the world is **so progressive and vibrant.**

I want you to think about what makes you different and please include all things that you think are both 'good' and 'bad'. To be honest, there is nothing bad about you; perhaps you are just a little quirky—and quirky is great! Again, it's what makes you, you!

If you were to compare answers with someone else, you would soon understand that we all have **different strengths and talents**. You might be great at sport but your friend might be an exceptional musician.

I REALLY WANT YOU TO EMBRACE THE FACT THAT THERE IS NOT ANOTHER YOU IN THIS WORLD. BE PROUD OF THAT!

At the end of the day, you could say we all have wings—we all have something to offer the world and to make ourselves soar. Please don't fret if you haven't found your wings yet! Just be open to **exploring**, and try to notice what you love to do and what you feel **passionate** about.

Sometimes, our wings can be for fighting for a cause or helping to solve a problem. They don't always have to revolve around a skill or talent. There are many examples of well-known people who have spoken openly about being 'unique' or 'different'. I'm pretty sure you have heard of Ed Sheeran? Did you know that as a child Ed had a terrible stutter (which is a speech problem) and was teased everyday due to that, and the fact that he had red hair and wore glasses? Yep, kids can be mean sometimes. Thankfully, Ed learnt to embrace his 'quirkiness' and decided to get involved in music at a pretty young age. As we all know, music became Ed's superpower, and he is now able to use his creativity to spread a positive message for us all. Ed has often been heard saying things like **embrace your weirdness** or just be yourself.

There are other well-known people that spread a similar message through their work. Lady Gaga has spoken about feeling different when she was young and eventually learning how to turn that into her strength. That's the trick; learning to turn your 'weirdness' into your strength.

It's pretty amazing how many people feel 'weird' at some point in their lives, or like they just don't fit in. I certainly did when I was younger. The truth is that many of us feel different because we are different, and that's exactly how it is meant to be! So the next time you feel like you are the 'odd one out', give yourself a pat on the back and know that you are on the right path; you are doing your own thing.

Walk your own path. Create your own adventure.

THINK DIFFERENTLY

When we learn to embrace ourselves as unique, we can start to appreciate that we are likely to think differently to our friends and family, and you know what? **That's a good thing.** Yes, we may want the same things as our friends and family such as love, happiness and to experience joy, but because we are all different on the inside, we will have a different way of doing things. So where one person sees a **problem,** you might see a **solution.** Or where someone tells you something can't be done, you might think to yourself, **'Well, I think I can do that.'** And these differences can actually be the sweet spot where the magic happens—it motivates you to get creative and take action and perhaps prove them all wrong!

The story of **Roger Bannister** is a great example.

The year was 1954 when a man named Roger Bannister achieved the 'impossible'. For many years, the 'experts' had said that it simply wasn't possible for a person to run four miles in under four minutes—they thought that the human body wasn't able to do it. Then on 6 May 1954, Roger actually achieved it. He ran four miles in three minutes and 59 seconds, and in doing so helped many others shift their thinking in terms of how fast they could run. Barely a year after Roger's success, someone else ran a mile in under four minutes, and then another and another. Today, it is not uncommon for people of all ages to run a four-minute mile. Roger showed others that the 'impossible' was **possible.**

By pushing himself to achieve his goal, he gave others permission to do the same. What is also so interesting about this story is that Roger Bannister said that he used visualisation to help him mentally prepare for his run!

SKY'S THE LIMIT

Just like the sky, creativity is limitless and that's the reason that the **world keeps changing.** Take a look around and observe what currently surrounds you, and think about this: everything you can see, other than nature, first started as an idea in somebody's mind.

The chair that you're sitting on;

The cup that you drink from;

The pen that you write with;

The clothes that you wear.

What else can you see right now? We are literally surrounded by other people's ideas that have been brought to life. **How cool is that?**

The reason that these physical items now exist is simply because someone at some time acted on their idea.

Now I'm guessing that you've had a few ideas over the years?

THE GREAT THING ABOUT IDEAS IS THEY DON'T HAVE A MINIMUM AGE REQUIREMENT.

They can come at any time and at any place. You might get an idea while you are having a shower or helping wash the car.

Start taking **notice of your ideas** because you just never know where they might lead you. An idea doesn't always have to lead to a new invention either. You might have an idea to go somewhere or talk to someone you wouldn't normally talk to. Just see if you can take notice of your ideas with a sense of wonder and see where they might lead you. Creativity is a wonderful thing and it's a really natural process.

 Once you tune in, you will see that ideas are everywhere!

THE GREAT IDEA

The bed that you sleep in,
that bed is for you.
But without it can I ask,
what would you do?

The pen that you write with,
that helps you take notes.
Without it just imagine,
how would you see what you wrote?

And have you ever had a thought
about the wheels on a car?
Without them you'd be stuck;
you certainly wouldn't go far.

From liquid paper to medicine;
the solutions appear.
When problems arise,
and are faced with courage not fear.

Inventors and scientists,
creators they are.
And what about musicians,
with sound that takes you afar?

The food on the table
is creativity in place.
The first woman on the moon?
Please watch this space!

Ideas lead to action,
and action into form.
And so, the idea itself
is where creativity is born.

And just like the Wright Brothers,
who invented the plane.
You need to have courage,
to help you survive the disdain.

'That can't be done'
they will tell you with fear.
But keep moving forward,
because lessons are near.

The mistakes as we go,
well they help us understand.
That things may start small,
before they grow grand.

So, take notice of your thoughts,
the crazy and weird.
For they are the great ones,
and may soon be revered.

Unleash your imagination;
please create and invent!
And in this great Universe,
you might just make a dent . . .

Creativity also helps us solve problems.

Just like it says in my poem: 'From liquid paper to medicine; the solutions appear. When problems arise, and are faced with courage; not fear.' At the end of the day, many things are created when we encounter a problem and are forced to think of a way to try and solve it. A recent example of this has to be the recent pandemic. On a global scale, humans faced a challenge and a pretty major one at that! Some people faced it with fear, while many other people faced it with creativity and awareness. Doctors, scientists, healthcare staff all looked for solutions. There were scientists and doctors working literally around the clock to try to come up with a vaccine, a medicine that could save lives. Even your family probably had to get creative as you all tried to figure out how to work together, in harmony, 24 hours a day!

This really goes back to our choices. Yes, there might be problems that we face, but remember that we can choose to stay stuck in fear, or we can choose to look for a solution. Can you choose to get creative and see how you can be part of the solution?

A PROBLEM IS JUST AN OPPORTUNITY TO GET CREATIVE!

LONG HAUL

We've already talked about **persistence**, which is about making a choice to keep going, even when you feel like giving up. When you've been onboard a long-haul flight, you have made a silent agreement with yourself to 'go the distance'. This means that you don't arrive at your stopover and think, **'I give up. I simply can't go any further.'** It's usually quite the opposite! You have set yourself the goal of arriving at a certain location and you are motivated to keep going until you get there. This, my friend, is the attitude of all the people who we have talked about so far.

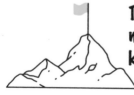

They had a dream, a vision or a mission for themselves and they kept going until they arrived at their destination.

Novak Djokovic had a dream of becoming the #1 tennis player in the world. **Dr Doty** visualised himself becoming a neurosurgeon. **Bethany Hamilton** believed her mission was to be a world champion surfer, even after losing her arm.

These **inspiring people** all had different dreams but do you know what they had in common?

THE COURAGE TO BELIEVE IN THEMSELVES AND TO KEEP MOVING FORWARD EVEN WHEN THINGS DIDN'T GO TO PLAN.

They were all determined to keep going with their journey.

There are so many great examples of people who have succeeded in their chosen field. I want you to start looking for stories that inspire you and help you believe that anything is possible. Learn to embrace your uniqueness and turn your dreams into reality.

YOU ARE THE ONE THAT YOU HAVE BEEN WAITING FOR!

REAL MAGIC

FOLLOWING THE FOLLOWERS

In my work, I see so many young people following the kids they think are 'cool'. That's not to say following them on social media, I mean trying to be like them. Usually these kids think they are 'cool' because they have the latest and greatest phone or because they act tough in the playground or think they are pretty good at something. What's important for you to recognise is that owning the latest iPhone doesn't mean they know what they are doing when it comes **to living their best life.** Or just because they have a loud voice, it doesn't make them any better than you. Or because they happen to be good at something, it doesn't mean that you don't have your own strengths and talents.

Don't make it a habit to follow the followers. These 'cool kids' appear to have it all sorted on the outside, but it doesn't necessarily mean that they do. They most likely enjoy the attention from everyone but have to work quite hard to keep it all up.

My hope is that you get to a point in your own journey where you don't want to follow anyone, that you are happy being you and proud of your quirkiness. But if you do want to take inspiration from someone, that's totally OK: just make sure the person that you take inspiration from is living their best life. What does that mean?

Take a close look at the person and ask yourself:

Is he/she a good person?

Is he/she spreading a positive message?

Is he/she setting a positive example to young people (and adults!)?

Is he/she attempting to make a positive difference in the world?

Seek out the role models who will help lift your spirits or who give you hope for a better world. But also start noticing the people who drain your energy or make you feel bad about yourself. They are simply not worth your time and energy!

FIND THE PEOPLE WHO MAKE YOUR HEART SING AND INSPIRE YOU TO SING YOUR OWN SONG.

FASTER, BIGGER, BETTER

Because the world is constantly changing, it means that there is always going to be a faster, bigger, better version of most things. Unfortunately, many of us get sucked in by the ads on TV telling us that this latest gadget is what we need to make us feel happy. I hate to break it to you, but it won't. Yes, you might get a little shopper high for 30 minutes or so after the purchase but trust me, the high won't last and it won't be long until you are craving the next thing.

You might have already experienced this. Think about the last time you really wanted something? It might have been the latest scooter or a new pair of trainers. I'm sure it felt pretty good when you got the new thing, yes? You may have felt excited or happy or a mixture of both. But can you remember how long that happiness lasted before the novelty of having the new thing faded away and you started thinking about the next thing that you wanted? Someone may have turned up to school in another pair of trainers that made yours seem like they weren't 'good enough' anymore? Or someone may have come along with a 'better' brand of scooter.

 **If we keep going like this, the chase never ends, and we never actually get to experience long-lasting happiness.**

SO WHAT DOES MAKE US HAPPY?

Thankfully, we have already thought about this—
happiness comes from the inside, not from the outside
things that we own or want. Have another look at our
selfies and think back to what they mean for you.
The truth is that when you really do love yourself
(self-love), you will begin to understand that it doesn't
matter what you have or own, because you feel good
regardless. Or when you are taking good care of
yourself (self-care), it doesn't matter if you don't have
the latest iPhone because you feel good anyway.

self-love   self-respect
self-determination   self-approval
self-belief   self-awareness   self-control
self-esteem   self-care   self-mastery

If you can make these things your focus every day,
then you are taking some pretty big steps in the right
direction. Yes, those external things can bring comfort
but at the end of the day, they will not make anyone
happy (even if the ads tell you otherwise!) If we
constantly make the 'stuff' our focus and we don't
have it, then that can lead to a never-ending feeling
of '**What about me?'**, which just doesn't feel good.

Choose to focus on what makes you feel good on the inside instead. **It really can be that simple!**

There are so many things that we can do for free (or relatively cheaply) that make us feel good anyway. Here's a few ideas . . .

swim in the ocean

laugh with a friend

listen to some uplifting music

do a random act of kindness for someone

go for a bushwalk and get into nature

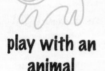
play with an animal

dance

sit in the morning sun and just breathe

go for a run

ABOVE AND BEYOND

In the same way external things, or a lack of having those external things, can make us question our worthiness, so can other people. Have you ever had a great idea that you shared with someone only to be told, **'That will never work'**? Or have you ever achieved something that you're really proud of only to be put down for your achievement by your so-called 'friends'?

Unfortunately, we are taught from a young age that we need to **compete** with each other and somehow prove our worthiness. Just think about when you sit an exam and then the results come out and everybody wants to know your score. You know why they want to know your score? To see if they beat you, of course! I've got to be honest with you, **it sucks.** There's no other way to say it. It really does suck that society teaches us to compete with each other rather than teaching us that we are OK just the way we are, and that we are all different.

So, let's get one thing straight: the only race you are in is one with yourself.

YOUR FOCUS SHOULD BE ON HOW YOU CAN BE BETTER THAN YOU WERE YESTERDAY.

Start by asking yourself this question every morning:

'How can I take myself
to the next level today?'

You can try something new or do something different
or give yourself permission to just be. If you need
a day of rest and relaxation, that is totally fine too.
Listen to your mind, body and spirit, and honour
what they are telling you. Don't worry about what
your friends are doing.

As for the people who are constantly putting you
down? **This is where you get to make a choice.**
You can try to play their game and run the risk of
feeling worse about yourself or you can choose to
take the high ground, which means that you simply
imagine yourself being like a plane and soaring
above and beyond their drama and negativity.

You can also move yourself away from them
physically so you literally don't waste your energy
on them. Your energy is a precious resource, so be
aware of how you are using it. Don't use it on people
who don't help you recharge. Protect your energy
and use it on the people and activities that make you
feel good.

TRAVEL VLOG

You have probably noticed that I have been pretty quiet on topic of social media and the internet so far on our journey together.

This has been quite deliberate as I really wanted to focus on the **superpowers within you** first. But I know how important this is in the lives of young people, so I feel the time has come to connect with this topic now.

I have no doubt in my mind that you are going to want to share your journey via a travel blog, a travel vlog or various other social media channels. That's totally fine but it's important to get a little knowledge in regards to all of this first. Over the years, I have heard many examples of things going wrong because people simply didn't think before they posted online or they didn't really understand the power of a post! So let's go there together now.

FOOTPRINTS

Every step we take leaves a footprint. You might not be able to see it unless you are walking on a beach, but the trail is still there. Social media is no different. Many of you might have already talked about this at school or with an adult, but it's important to be aware of what happens when you post on social media. You start leaving 'social media footprints'.

Say, for example, that you have an argument with a friend at school. You get home and while you are online, she shares something that happened throughout the day. Without giving it too much thought, you post a not-so-nice comment: **'You think you're so cool,'** or something like that. You do this because you are still angry and it's easier to say something mean online than it is to say it in person.

About an hour later, you go back online and now other people have commented on your post and you start to feel terrible. You delete your comment but you know it's too late because your friend will have already seen it.

Your inner critic starts up: **'Why did you do that?'**

This is one of the greatest challenges you face when it comes to sharing online. It can all happen so quickly and it's easy to get caught up in the speed of it all. Many people don't stop to think before they hit 'POST' or 'SHARE'. You also need to be aware that whatever you share, like or comment on will be there permanently and this how a digital footprint is created. You might think that you have deleted comments or items from your profile, as they are no longer visible to you, but they still exist and can be accessed if needed.

What does this actually mean? It means that the things you post when you are 12, 15 or 18 years old will be still be accessible when you are 25 or 30. It basically sits out there indefinitely. So remember to:

 **PAUSE B4U POST.**

Please stop and think things through before you hit the 'SHARE' button. Take some time and ask yourself a few questions before you press anything:

1. Would I feel comfortable saying this to a person face to face?

2. Could there be any negative consequences if I post this?

3. Is this something I want to have a record of?

4. Is this helpful to myself and others?

STAYING IN TOUCH

There is no doubt about it, social media is great way of staying in touch with people, particularly people who live overseas or you don't see on a daily basis. However, many of us are getting lost in the digital world and we are forgetting to stay in touch with the real world! This means connecting with real people and having real experiences because this is actually where the real magic happens.

Think about it this way. You might be scrolling thorough Instagram and see a picture of the most colourful, delectable ice-cream that you have ever seen. **How does it make you feel?** It might make you want an ice-cream. On some level, you know that the experience of actually eating the ice-cream is way better then looking at someone else's picture of one. We are born with five senses:

TASTE, TOUCH, SMELL, SIGHT AND SOUND

And we feel most alive when we are using all five of our senses. Think about that ice-cream again. When you see it on Instagram, you are using one sense, sight. But when you eat that ice-cream in reality, you are using all five senses and this is what makes the ice-cream so darn good!

You can even go one step further and really **savour** that experience and you will literally create new neural pathways in your brain.

NOW THAT IS REAL MAGIC!

JUST BREATHE

AIRPLANE MODE

Ahhh, airplane mode. The smartphone function that thousands of people dislike **but** the introvert in me seriously loves! It's like a forced shutdown period for many, which is why they aren't fans.

A big part of the journey for you will be learning how to manage without technology. I totally understand that technology is entertaining and it keeps you occupied when you are **'bored'**, but if you are always on technology, when do you get a chance to check in with how you are really feeling? The answer for many of you is that you simply don't.

Like we talked about earlier, it's OK to feel sadness, it's OK to feel disappointment and other challenging emotions, and the faster we know that we feel this way, the faster we will move back into a neutral state. When we ignore our feelings or distract ourselves with technology, those feelings can become our **excess baggage** that we carry with us everywhere.

REMEMBER that excess baggage we talked about earlier?

Something else can also happen if we are always distracting ourselves with technology.

226

Have you ever felt physically tired at the end of the day and jumped into bed feeling **totally exhausted** but when your head hits the pillow, it's like your mind wakes up? Your mind might want you to think about this problem and that problem and you find yourself just lying there, thinking.

Why does this happen? My theory is that it's usually the first opportunity that you have given yourself to just be. Your mind isn't distracted anymore by TV or smart devices, or other activities and it's like a nice pocket of space just opens up for you when you climb into bed.

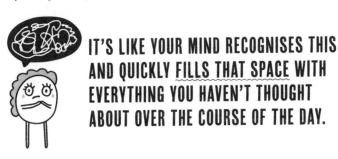

IT'S LIKE YOUR MIND RECOGNISES THIS AND QUICKLY FILLS THAT SPACE WITH EVERYTHING YOU HAVEN'T THOUGHT ABOUT OVER THE COURSE OF THE DAY.

And when you are lying there in your bed, these problems might seem worse because you are there on your own. Does that make sense?

This is why it's so important to give ourselves some mental space throughout the course of our day. That is where meditation or simply just sitting with our breath becomes so helpful. This is your airplane mode.

All you need to do is find ten minutes and switch off from technology, people or anything else that is going to distract you and just choose to connect with yourself. In other words:

Disconnect to reconnect.

During this time, you might like to do the practice what we talked about earlier to check in with yourself and see what is happening on the inside. Simply ask yourself the questions below and see what answers you receive.

'My mind feels . . .?'

'My body feels . . .?'

'My spirit feels . . .?'

Make it a habit to regularly ask yourself how you are doing, just like you would a good friend. And on days that you aren't feeling great, ask yourself, 'What do I need to do right now?' and give yourself permission to listen to the answer.

This is where you might like to go back to your **self-care plan** and see what actions you could take to help yourself feel better. It might be something as easy as drinking a glass of water or taking a shower.

Or even just sitting with your breath.

I know you probably haven't been counting, but do you know I have mentioned the words breath or breathing more than 50 times in this book? Before our journey comes to end, I'll let you know why it is so important and why I keep going on about it!

DEEP BREATHS ARE LIKE HITTING THE PAUSE BUTTON.

THE POWER OF THE BREATH

Do you know what the coolest thing about your breath is? It is always with you. We literally need our breath to keep us alive.

When we learn to pay attention to our breath, it can help to bring us into the present moment. Another way to think about this is that your breath cannot be in yesterday nor can it be in tomorrow. It can only be in this moment.

When you choose to tune into your breath, your mind slows down and connects with the present moment.

Another great thing about your breath is that when you take **conscious breaths,** it's like pressing the pause button on your nervous system, like we talked about earlier. This is why you've probably heard people say 'take three deep breaths' before an exam or a performance, because in doing that, you can literally calm your body and brain down.

Just so you realise how important your breathing is, I want to share some advice from someone who now travels the world teaching people how to breathe properly. Yep, you read that correctly, Dan Brule literally teaches people how to breathe and so it's now time for episode no. 9.

KEEP CALM &...

Breathe

UP AND AWAY
with DAN BRULE

Dan Brule is known as the Bruce Lee of breathing. Bruce Lee was 'the' master when it came to martial arts and Dan is the pretty much the master of breath. He travels around the world teaching people how to breathe well because, truth be told, many of us don't breathe as effectively as we could. He has taught Navy SEALs, Olympic athletes, business leaders and everyday people like you and me. He has literally taught thousands of people how to improve their health and performance by working with their breath. Dan says:

Remember to stop and take a conscious breath, to feel ourselves open and expand with the inhale and relax and let go with the exhale.

If we can remember and choose to do this in certain moments, it can make all the difference in the world!

Dan is also part of the International Breathwork Foundation, an organisation dedicated to teaching people how to breathe, properly. If I asked you to remember a time when you know you weren't breathing properly, my guess is that you would probably be able to think of a few times? It might have been a time when you were nervous or scared.

Can you remember how your breathing changed?

It was most likely shallow breathing, like taking short gasps of air or even holding your breath? To take a proper breath, we need to try to remember to send our breath right down into our belly, until our belly expands like a balloon.

Go on, try it now!

Dan has also helped to create a program for students called **The Breathing Classroom** and was happy to share some of their breathing techniques.

ARTIST BREATH

Breathe in and out deeply and imagine breathing into your arms or hands before you draw or paint or work with clay.

CALMING BREATH

Double up on the exhale! Breathe in for two counts and then out for four counts. For older children you can inhale for three counts and exhale for six counts.

ATHLETE'S BREATH

Breathe in deeply and imagine sending breaths down into your legs if you are about to run or jump. Breathe into your arms if you are about to throw a ball!

BUNNY BREATH

This breath can help children through crying. It follows the natural rhythm of a child's cry. Get them to do three short sniffs through the nose, and a longer exhale through the mouth.

THE ADVENTURE BEGINS

PERSONAL DEVICE

Hopefully you now understand that external things might bring fleeting moments of joy and provide comfort but very rarely provide us with long-term happiness. This includes your smartphone. Yes, it may provide you with hours of entertainment but that is purely distraction, which may have its place, but is it really helping you take your life to the next level?

IF YOU CAN PUT YOUR PHONE DOWN, IT GIVES YOU THE OPPORTUNITY TO CONNECT WITH THE GREATEST PERSONAL DEVICE YOU WILL EVER HAVE: YOU!

Can you put away the external distractions and start to get to know who you truly are and what is happening on the inside?

For example, what makes you happy? What makes you angry? Remember all these feelings are there for a reason. Anger might be signalling that a boundary has been crossed. Excitement might be an indication to **keep going** and boredom may be a **wake-up call?** Maybe you are being called to create something.

233

Let's revisit our check-in practice.

Start by taking a nice big breath in through your nose and out through the mouth and give yourself permission to relax.

Allow yourself to find a nice neutral spot and when you feel comfortable and relaxed, ask yourself these three questions:

1 *My mind needs . . .?*

2 *My body needs . . .?*

3 *My spirit needs . . .?*

Remain open and curious to any answers you might receive. Come back to your breathing and when you are ready, open your eyes.

You might like to make a note of anything that came up for you during that practice. What does your mind, body and spirit need in this moment?

CABIN FEVER

At this point in the journey, you might be getting a little bit of **cabin fever**. That is, you want to get moving but not quite sure of what to do next. Maybe you're feeling a little overwhelmed with all this information that you've been given? My advice is to keep focused just on your next step.

What is the next right action you can take that will guide you towards your mission or goal?

If you really were coming off a long-haul flight, the first thing you might like to do is have a big stretch and get yourself grounded.

LET YOUR FEET TOUCH THE GROUND AND BREATHE.

The next step doesn't have to be a big step; it could be little steps that will still have you moving in the right direction. Remember, it's about consistency rather than intensity. For example, if you want to improve your presentation skills, you might start by giving a talk to your mum or dad in the living room. You wouldn't necessarily go out and present at a whole school assembly straight away! Start small and build it up. The most important thing is to: Stick with it!

So many people give up after a few days of trying because they haven't seen any results and they think it isn't working. Remember the pilot who turns the jumbo jet left? The jumbo jet doesn't turn left straight away, it takes a bit of time. **Real change takes time.**

IT'S AMAZING WHAT WE CAN ACHIEVE WHEN WE CHOOSE TO STICK WITH IT.

HIT THE GROUND RUNNING

When that plane finally hits the tarmac,
you want to hit the ground running.
What does that mean?

HIT THE GROUND RUNNING

to immediately work hard and successfully at a new activity.

It simply means to take action! Use all this new information to your advantage and embrace this exciting time in your life. You are literally opening the doors to change.

What do you want to see on the other side of the doors? Problems or possibilities? Remember that it's OK to create the best-case scenario for yourself. Breathe into any anxiety that you might feel and turn it into excitement instead. You can even start calling it **anxcitement!**

ANXCITEMENT:
A feeling of both anxiety and excitement.

DISCOVERY

There is so much for you to discover and I am so excited for you. It will soon be time for you to get unpacked and truly get started on your odyssey. Can you remember what we packed? Here's a little reminder:

COURAGE   OPEN MIND

WILLINGNESS TO TRY   **PERSISTENCE**

CURIOSITY   GRATITUDE

SELF-LOVE

If you can make use of these **special items** as you go through your days, you really are going to go places. Is there anything else that you have learnt along the way that you would like to add?

Head to your diary and list anything else that you have picked up in our journey together. For example:

Fear = feedback.

Have courage to try new things.

Treat yourself like your own best friend.

BEGINNINGS

As we come to the end of our journey together, it's really just the beginning for you.

I hope that you are also **beginning** to understand that your life really is an adventure and you get to decide how it goes from here.

You have your whole life in front of you, so begin to live it with **wonder, joy** and a sense of **awe.** It's OK to feel good and it's OK to have dreams for yourself. Please, dream away!

I would like to share one more **UP AND AWAY** episode with you before we officially come to the end. I have deliberately left this amazing person until last because her story so nicely sums up everything that we have spoken about throughout this book:

courage ⭐ persistence ⭐ self-belief ⭐ determination ⭐ being different

UP AND AWAY

with MICHELLE PAYNE

Michelle was the first woman to win the Melbourne Cup horse race, the biggest horse race in Australia, riding the Prince of Penzance. If you have read her book *Life As I Know It* or seen the movie *Ride Like a Girl*, you will be familiar with Michelle's incredible story and all the obstacles that she overcame before she fulfilled her dream. Not only had Michelle lost her mother and sister, she also overcame major injury and experienced many challenges as a woman competing in a male-dominated sport. Despite all these challenges, Michelle kept moving forward, and she did so with courage and humility.

Q. You have overcome a lot of challenges to be where you are today. Did you ever feel like giving up?

A. Yes. There were many times doubt crept into my mind. Certainly, there were times during my career where I seemed to be going nowhere. My injuries weren't always times of giving up or huge setbacks, they were times of taking a step back and thinking of ways to be able to put more into preparing to achieve my dreams. Unfortunately, a part of achieving my goal meant being a little selfish and I kept to myself a lot. This was my way of making sure I had no distractions in being able to put in everything in to being the best I could be. There were times where I would have a bad run; basically everything seemed to go wrong. One time, I went three months without riding a winner. The main thing I remember thinking was that I just had to keep showing up and doing my absolute best. I had to recognise that eventually it would change and it did.

Q. What are the biggest lessons that you have learnt when dealing with some of the challenges that you have faced?

A. One of the biggest lessons I have learnt is to surround yourself with good, positive people. Negative people can be very difficult and make life so much harder. I think be as kind as you can to those people who bring you down, but distance yourself as much as you can from their negativity as it can be very powerful.

Q. You knew from a young age that you wanted to be a jockey and your story will continue to inspire many people, particularly young females. What advice do you have for young people about 'daring to be different'?

A. There will be times when walking into a crowd feels very daunting—you may feel people looking at you, but hold your head high. You deserve to be there just as much as everyone else. I guess in a way I used people's judgement to make me want to prove them wrong and try even harder.

Q. Any tips that you can share in regards to not giving up on your dream?

A. I think a big problem that many people face is their fear of failure. You can't be afraid to fail because there will be times where you will get it wrong despite doing your absolute best. Learn from these times and understand that everyone makes mistakes.

Q. In this book, we have talked a lot about the power of meditation and visualisation. Did you use either of these tools as part of your training before winning the Melbourne Cup?

A. I visualise a lot of the races in my head going into a race and how I suspect the race will pan out and unfold. I find when the time comes to making split-second decisions in a race, I am more prepared.

Let Michelle's advice inspire you. You don't have to wait for someone else's permission to go out there and live the life of your dreams. Actually, don't waste your time waiting for someone else to give you permission, because you may never receive it! You already have everything you need.

THE WORLD IS WAITING FOR YOU!

Always remember that there is no one else in the world like you, and that is your superpower. Find out what makes you different and go with it. Know that you can and will contribute in your own special way and that the world needs you. It really, genuinely does!

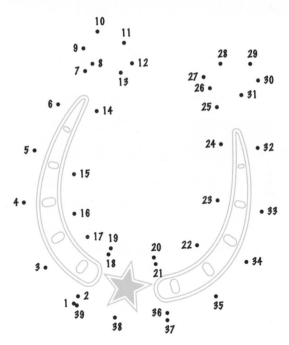

'One of the biggest lessons I have learnt is to surround yourself with good, positive people.'

— Michelle Payne

TIME TO SHINE!

STAY SEATED

I know, I know, you just want to be on your way now. But we haven't quite finished yet! There are just a few final points that I would like you to ponder once you leave the plane.

1) **YOUR BEAUTIFUL SELF:** There is only one you, so take good care of yourself. Be kind, patient and treat yourself well. When you feel good, you will find it easy to do good in this world of ours. Self-care is not selfish—it should be your priority.

2) **BE A FORCE FOR GOOD:** Whatever it is that you choose to do, please be a force for good. This means making a choice every day to contribute in a positive way to your life, the lives of others and the world. Believe that you can make a positive difference and you will.

3) **STAY HUMBLE:** Have you ever been around a person that just brags and brags? How does it make you feel? I am guessing not great. Every time someone brags it's like they are adding a brick to a brick wall and that wall is being built smack bang in the middle of

your relationship! Bragging is not the way to make friends or impress people. Just be you! If you are good at something, let your actions speak for themselves. People will soon be able to see it for themselves—you don't need to shout it from the rooftops.

4 **YOU ARE EXACTLY WHERE YOU ARE MEANT TO BE:** It doesn't matter where your current destination is, just know that you are exactly where you are meant to be. Yes, your best friend might be further along and that's great for him or her, but they have a different journey to make. Just accept that we all have different routes and give yourself a pat on the back for getting to where you are.

Now, this last point deserves its own heading. I actually wish I could write it in the sky for you:

YOU'VE GOT THIS!

Whatever happens from here, please remember that you **have got this**. You really do.

Inside your heart is everything that you need. You just have to learn to quieten your mind so that you can hear it. Let your heart guide you, and you will arrive at your destination.

Yes, there may be detours.

Yes, there may be some turbulence along the way, but you are stronger than you think.

The human spirit is resilient and it can keep going despite the challenges. Remember that everything that happens is really happening to help you grow and learn, and to help you become the best person that you can possibly be.

And in case no one has told you lately, I believe in you and I love you for being the person that you are. I see you, and:

it's time that everyone else gets to see your LIGHT SHINE!

THE ULTIMATE DESTINATION

If you really want to know where the ultimate destination is, this has to be it. It's a place that I named **GREATFULNESS** and it's actually a place that is found within you and is accessed through your imagination. To the person who hasn't visited Greatfulness yet, let me explain where it is.

I discovered this place for myself through regular meditation. Actually, you could say that meditation is the key to getting there and it's the reason why I created the Greatfulness program: because I really want to teach you how to get there.

This is a place like no other.

Greatfulness is a feeling of being in love with your life. It's a magical place where you can expect the unexpected and look forward to a wonderful adventure every day. When you discover Greatfulness, everything and anything becomes possible.

When you find this place, you literally forget about yourself and connect with something so much bigger. Everything seems to flow and you will simply observe that your dreams are well and truly alive inside you.

You feel full of love and this love fills you with an energy that is out of this world! Once you have found this lovely place, you begin to understand that a big part of your mission is actually helping other people discover this magical location for themselves.

So how do you get there? You start by simply closing your eyes and letting go. When you can let go of all the thoughts and the distractions, that's when you will find this point within and you can stay for as long as you like. When you come back to this time and space, you begin to realise that all of the external stuff will never, ever bring you the same feeling that Greatfulness does. A sense of peace, love and of wholeness.

You can have, be or do anything in Greatfulness: it is a place of unlimited possibilities. It took me more than 40 years to find this place but I am so pleased I never gave up the search. You see, what I was seeking was within me all of the time—I just didn't have the guidebook.

You now have the guidebook within your hands and trust me, if you follow the advice in this book, your life will be full of wonder, magic and miracles.

So now it is time for us to say goodbye. Enjoy your travels and please don't forget to send me a postcard.

With love and gratitude,
Jacqui xx

THE REAL JOURNEY STARTS WITHIN

END NOTE

A FINAL WORD AND RECOMMENDED RESOURCES

Throughout this book you have been introduced to different ways of thinking, feeling and being. However, there are going to be times when you might feel 'stuck in a rut'. I just want to assure you that we all have bad days. All of us experience moments in our lives when things don't seem to go to plan or we get stuck in a cycle of negative thinking. It's important to remember that you are not alone. If, at any time, you feel like your thoughts are not helping you then never be afraid to reach out for help. There are many professional people out there who can and will help you. You can try some of the tools in this book but if you feel like nothing is helping you to feel better, then I really do advise talking to a professional. Being a human can be tricky and even painful at times but I truly believe that we are not meant to suffer in silence. Talk about your experience and get the help you need to work through what is happening. I have learnt, from my own personal experience, that sharing your load with someone else can really help.

If you would like to reach out for some help, here are some wonderful resources that I recommend:

Kids Helpline **1800 55 1800** *kidshelpline.com.au*
(telephone and online counselling for ages 5–25)

Lifeline **13 11 14** *lifeline.org.au*

Headspace *headspace.org.au*
(eheadspace to chat online)

SANE Australia **1800 18 7263** *sane.org*

ReachOut.com *au.reachout.com*
(youth mental health service)

Beyond Blue *beyondblue.org.au*

Black Dog Institute
blackdoginstitute.org.au

RUOK *ruok.org.au*

For those of you who would like some help getting started with meditation, these are my recommended apps:

calm.com
smilingmind.com.au
headspace.com

OTHER RESOURCES

Jacqueline Jones *greatfulness.com.au*
If you visit my website you will be able to access free activities and 'Headventures' to get you started on your journey. Enjoy!

 Read more about the people mentioned in this book to help you stay inspired!

Andy McCann *dnadefinitive.com*

Bethany Hamilton *bethanyhamilton.com*

Chloe Logarzo *instagram.com/chloelogarzo*

Dan Brule *breathmastery.com*

Dr James R. Doty *intothemagicshop.com*

Isaiah Dawe *idknowyourself.com*

Mel Robbins *melrobbins.com*

Michelle Payne *michellejpayne.com.au*

Novak Djokovic *novakdjokovic.com/en/*

Ryan Hrljeac *ryanswell.ca*

Wright Brothers *wright-brothers.org*

Susan Cain *quietrev.com*

Tom Cronin *tomcronin.com/meditation*

GLOSSARY

Analogy *noun*
1. An agreement, likeness, or correspondence between the relations of things to one another; a partial similarity in particular circumstances on which a comparison may be based.
2. Agreement; similarity.
IN MY WORDS: when you compare two things that are different but have some things in common. I use the analogy of travel in this book to help me explain the power of the mind and how you can truly flourish in life.

Conscious *adjective*
1. Aware of one's own existence, sensations, cognitions, etc.; endowed with consciousness.
2. Inwardly sensible or awake to something.
IN MY WORDS: aware of who you are as a whole person; mind, body and spirit.

Depression *noun*
1. Depression is more than just a low mood—it's a serious condition that affects your physical and mental health (taken from BeyondBlue: beyondblue.org.au/the-facts/depression).
IN MY WORDS: a feeling of sadness that you can't seem to get rid of, no matter what you try.

Extrovert *noun*
1. Someone characterised by extroversion; someone concerned chiefly with what is external or objective.
2. To direct (the mind, etc.) outwards, or to things outside the self.
IN MY WORDS: someone who is drawn to the external world and who gets their energy from other people.

Introvert *noun*
1. Someone characterised by introversion; someone concerned chiefly with their own thoughts.
2. To turn inwards.
IN MY WORDS: someone who is drawn to their inner world of thoughts and feelings rather than other people. Introverts get their energy from going 'within' themselves.

Intuition *noun*
1. Direct perception of truths, facts, etc., independently of any reasoning process.
2. A truth or fact thus perceived.
3. The ability to perceive in this way.
IN MY WORDS: a truth that is felt inside the body. Some people call it a 'gut feeling' because many people feel it in their stomach area. It is like our inner compass or inner 'knowing'.

Mental Health *noun*
1. A condition in which mental functions are successfully performed and there is no mental illness.
IN MY WORDS: a healthy mind that works well and is free from illness.

Neuroplasticity *noun*
1. The ability of the brain to change, both in physical structure and in functional organisation, in response to experience.
IN MY WORDS: the power to rewire your brain.

Neutral *noun*
1. An impartial or unbiased state or person.
IN MY WORDS: when you reach neutral point or zero it is a feeling of 'just being'. You don't feel caught up in negative or positive feelings or thoughts. It's a bit like reaching home base in a game of tip. You know you don't have to do anything and that you are safe. You simply 'are'.

Odyssey *noun*
1. Any long series of wanderings.
IN MY WORDS: a glorious adventure!

Remedy *noun*
1. Something that cures or relieves a disease or bodily disorder; a healing medicine, application, or treatment.
IN MY WORDS: a successful way of dealing with a problem.

Resilience *noun*
1. Resilient power; elasticity.
2. Resilient action; rebound; recoil.
3. Power of ready recovery from sickness, depression, or the like; buoyancy; cheerfulness.
IN MY WORDS: a person's ability to bounce back from challenges or when things don't go as planned. You might feel 'knocked over' butyou get back up and keep going.

Ripple Effect *noun* (taken from Cambridge online dictionary)
1. A situation in which one event produces effects which spread and produce further effects.
IN MY WORDS: when your action or words make an impact on those around you. This can be positive or negative.

THE 'SELFIES'

• **Self-approval** *noun*
1. Approval of oneself.
IN MY WORDS: accepting yourself as you are.

• **Self-awareness** *noun*
1. Conscious knowledge of one's own character and feelings.
IN MY WORDS: Knowing yourself. Understanding your strengths and weaknesses and being aware of your thoughts, feelings and behaviour.

Self-belief *noun*
1. Confidence in the rightness of one's own ideas and beliefs.
IN MY WORDS: confidence in yourself.

Self-care *noun*
1. The practice of taking action to preserve or improve one's own health.
IN MY WORDS: Looking after your mind, body and spirit.

Self-control *noun*
1. Control of oneself or one's actions, feelings, etc.
IN MY WORDS: being able to manage yourself well.

Self-determination *noun*
1. Determination by oneself or itself, without outside influence.
IN MY WORDS: believing in yourself and not stopping until you reach your goals.

Self-esteem *noun*
1. One's sense of one's own worth.
IN MY WORDS: seeing the good in yourself. Feeling proud of yourself.

Self-love *noun*
1. Care that that constitutes one's proper relation with oneself.
IN MY WORDS: appreciating being you. Treating yourself like you would your best friend.

Self-mastery *noun*
1. Self-control.
IN MY WORDS: Trusting yourself and knowing that no matter what happens: 'You have got this!'

Self-respect *noun*
1. Proper esteem or regard for the dignity of one's character.
IN MY WORDS: sticking up for yourself. Knowing what is right and wrong for you.

WHAT PEOPLE ARE SAYING ABOUT GREATFULNESS

Students

'The most useful information I have ever been taught.'

'She was always happy and was really encouraging and told us amazing stories. And it was a good thing that Mrs Jones does it because she has had depression and I know she is trying to help everyone to skip what she went through and I feel so privileged that she is fighting for us.'

'We learnt how to accomplish our goals and how to be the person we want to be in the future.'

'It helped me to realise what I love to do and what makes me happy. It made me feel good about myself and helped me to realise how special I am.'

'Mrs Jones taught me that it's OK to be different.'

Parents

'Reading this book with my two boys (aged 12 and 10) was such a joyful experience. Many nights we would cuddle up on the couch, read a few chapters and have an amazing discussion about what we have just learnt. My boys really absorbed the content, finding the travel idea really easy to relate to. This book will be re-read many times in my household, as it's packed with unlimited skills, possibilities and so much personal discovery. A beautiful book and such an important read, especially in today's busy world.'

'I was really impressed by you, Jacqui, the openness of your own mental health battle and the work you are doing with all parts of the community is inspiring. We are so lucky to be part of a school community that values the mental health of its students and that it is part of the education received. If only these types of programs were available when I was at school. It's wonderful that we can talk openly about mental health and encourage those around us to do the same. I congratulate you for being such a passionate advocate for children's wellbeing and thank you again for the session and work you're doing with our children.'

'I would highly recommend it as a strong support for the entire family's mental health. We live in such a busy world and it can be stressful, and this session really inspires a positive way of creating healthy habits and mindset change for good mental health.'

Teachers

'The students, staff and parents of our community have all benefited from the programs that Jacqui Jones has brought to our school. 'Greatfulness' has helped our students to develop a variety of important life skills. These include being reflective, demonstrating empathy, being resilient, being grateful and being respectful towards self and others. Many parents have commented on the positive impact that these programs have had on their children. Thank you.'

– Daniel (Assistant Principal)

'I loved *The Greatfulness Guide*—how I wish as a young person someone had shared the power of thinking this way with me! The interviews and studies of eminent people provided real examples of how regular people can achieve and become amazing things once they set their mind to it. The journey this book takes you on is a real adventure for the mind and the guide is fun and simple to follow.'

– Nicole (School Principal)

MY IDEAS

MY IDEAS

 **MY IDEAS**

 # MY IDEAS